ArtScroll® Series

Rabbi Nosson Scherman / Rabbi Meir Zlotowitz

General Editors

Published by

Mesorah Publications, ltd

RABBI NOACH ORLOWEK

Turning Ideas into Action

FIRST EDITION
First Impression … July 2013

Published and Distributed by
MESORAH PUBLICATIONS, LTD.
4401 Second Avenue / Brooklyn, N.Y 11232

Distributed in Europe by
LEHMANNS
Unit E, Viking Business Park
Rolling Mill Road
Jarow, Tyne & Wear, NE32 3DP
England

Distributed in Australia and New Zealand
by **GOLDS WORLDS OF JUDAICA**
3-13 William Street
Balaclava, Melbourne 3183
Victoria, Australia

Distributed in Israel by
SIFRIATI / A. GITLER — BOOKS
6 Hayarkon Street
Bnei Brak 51127, Israel

Distributed in South Africa by
KOLLEL BOOKSHOP
Northfield Centre, 17 Northfield Avenue
Glenhazel 2192, Johannesburg, South Africa

ARTSCROLL® SERIES
TURNING IDEAS INTO ACTION
© *Copyright 2013, by* MESORAH PUBLICATIONS, Ltd.
4401 Second Avenue / Brooklyn, N.Y. 11232 / (718) 921-9000 / www.artscroll.com

---

ISBN 10: 1-4226-1403-4 / ISBN 13: 978-1-4226-1403-7

Typography by CompuScribe at ArtScroll Studios, Ltd.

Printed in the United States of America
Bound by Sefercraft, Quality Bookbinders, Ltd., Brooklyn N.Y. 11232

*I*n loving memory of our dear mother,
grandmother, and great-grandmother

שפרה בת יצחק
נפ׳ ח׳ סיון תשע״ב

A woman of integrity, with a kind smile and a gentle touch, whose greatest delight was to spend time with her family.

We learn from Yaakov Avinu that a tzaddik values his possessions, no matter how big or small. The value is not intrinsic, but rather the tzaddik wishes to use the material item as a tool in his service of Hashem. A tzaddik acknowledges the effort required to take possession of an item. So did our mother, grandmother, and great-grandmother know how to value things properly.

May we all be zocheh to learn from her teachings the importance of family, the caring for an item no matter its financial value, the insight of knowing where to spend our time and whom to spend it with.

We miss you.

RABBI SIMCHA SCHEINBERG
Rosh HaYeshiva Yeshivas Torah Ore

הרב שמחה שיינברג
ראש הישיבה ישיבת תורה אור ירושלים
בן מרן רבי חיים פינחס שיינברג זצוק"ל

ב"ה ל' לאדר"ח ולשמחה וליראה שי"ג נפשי
הגאון הרב נח אורלוויק שליט"א מאשין
ב'שבתינו הק' צוות להוצאה ולהדפיס
של הדרכה בדרכי צוות דרך
בלי המינוך הנ"א בברם - הגאון האחד
אברך להסכמ ב של' היון כבר מלוהם
לזולת כמותה האון וענני' חינוך והגדה
וישלו הלבשה רחה האון היוך מגאלא'פ
ה אינ הק"ק שלא דין נפשנו לאלוו ישנו
בדור ובברקין מכני דרכה בר.
שמענו ודענע לוזר מוס ל רכה המרין
שהספר הזה ישגא מסתוא לחוויר
הורים והתמנכים ב"ה דו'כם לתאית
הקוש לאורדרכה רצאן וירכה הראשון
רצוגא ודולה הראן תורה ולהאן ויק
שמוך מעותה הנפש והרחות הצע כל

הנוח חל תמונ וש"ם
ראין התורה אוי ויל
שמחה שיינברג

6 Panim Merot Street• Jerusalem, PO Box 6967 • 02.537.2928
רחוב פנים מאירות 6 ירושלים ת.ד. 6979 טל.02.537.2928 ישראל

Table Of Contents

▷ Chapter 6: GETTING THE MOST OUT OF LIFE

A short note of appreciation for Mori V'Rabi HaGaon Rosh HaYeshivah HaRav Chaim Pinchus Scheinberg, zt"l

On 27 Adar 5772 the Rosh Yeshivah, *zt"l*, Mori V'Rabi Ha-Gaon HaRav Chaim Pinchus Scheinberg, *zt"l*, left this world. He is very much alive in the minds of his *talmidim*, but the loss is searing and pervasive in those who took his life teachings to heart. It is of no help to us that he lived to be exactly 101½, just as it is of no help to say that we had the Beis HaMikdash for 410 years. The loss is irreparable, for even when he was old and frail, his very presence could evoke growth and inspiration.

About a year before his *petirah*, I was an eyewitness to something unforgettable. The Rosh Yeshivah would daven in his house, and then he would come to the yeshivah to daven from the beginning of *chazaras hashatz*. After davening, he fell fast asleep in his chair. He was tired, and he had a right to be tired. After all, he was almost 100 years old!

His loyal caretaker, Reb Yehudah Solomon, tried to wake him in order to transfer him to his wheelchair. "Rebbe, Rebbe," he'd repeat several times, to no avail; the Rosh Yeshivah was fast asleep. Then Reb Yehudah hit on an ingenious idea. "Rebbe," he said, "it's time to say *shiur*."[1] The Rosh Yeshivah immediately stood up and extended his hands in order to be supported the few steps to his wheelchair, so that he could be taken to where he would give the *shiur*.

Afterward, Reb Yehudah told me that in the last period of the Rosh Yeshivah's life, Reb Yehudah, then unmarried, would sleep in the apartment with the Rosh Yeshivah. Often, the Rosh Yeshivah would awaken several times in the night for fear of missing *vasikin* (the sunrise *minyan*). When the morning did arrive, he was often fast asleep. Reb Yehudah would try to wake him up, often without success, until he whispered in his ear, "It's time for *vasikin*." At that, the Rosh Yeshivah would immediately arise and get ready for a new, full day of *avodas Hashem* and Torah study.

His *kedushah* and closeness to Hashem during those last years was evident to everyone — because he couldn't make the effort to conceal it. But there were times when he knew that he could affect others only by consciously sharing his fear and love of Hashem, and he did so. HaGaon Rav Yosef Stern, *shlita*, a *gadol b'Torah* who has been in the yeshivah since its earliest years in Eretz Yisrael, pointed out this ability to be able to reach anyone when he related to me the following stories.

The Rosh Yeshivah had been asked to attend a bar mitzvah meal of a particular class that was unusually difficult to manage and quite turned off to the study of Torah. The fact that they were in a school specifically geared to their needs, and that their teachers were dedicated to them, didn't seem to be having the desired effect.

---

1. For many decades, the Rosh Yeshivah would say a *Mishnah Berurah shiur* every day. During his last years, someone would read the *Mishnah Berurah*, and he would comment or answer questions.

Toward the end of the meal, the Rosh Yeshivah began to sing, "*Lulei Torascha sha'ashu'ai az avadeti b'anyi...* — If not for Your Torah, which is my joy, then I would have become lost in my sorrow..." and tears streamed from his eyes. The children began to sing with him, and they, too, began to cry. The school said that the class became a changed group and from then on began learning with a fresh enthusiasm that left their teachers dumbfounded.

The same thing happened when the Rosh Yeshivah was asked to inspire a group of teenagers. There were several hundred students in the room, and the Rosh Yeshivah began singing. There wasn't a dry eye in the room as the students joined in for an unforgettable, once-in-a-lifetime connection to someone whose heart and mind were immutably connected to Torah.

The Rosh Yeshivah taught, through word and deed, the enormous importance of using time properly, especially for Torah study. If the clock in the *beis midrash* was slow, he would never let it be set ahead until the study period had ended. Time was not to be deducted from *seder*, even just to reset a clock.

I remember when I made a bris for my son in the yeshivah. It was on a Friday. and the mohel said it would have to be done at 9 a.m. The Rosh Yeshivah was unhappy about the time, which was during the learning *seder*, and said it should be done at noon, when the Friday *seder* ended. The mohel was adamant and insisted on the 9 a.m. time. The Rosh Yeshivah didn't like it, but did not oppose him.

Nine a.m. came. The mohel looked at the child and said that the child was yellow and he would not perform the bris. The Rosh Yeshivah looked at the child, didn't agree that the child was yellow and asked for Yossele, the famous Yerushalmi mohel, to come and examine the child. Out of respect for the Rosh Yeshivah, Yossele agreed to come, but first he needed to finish his daily round of brisos. He finally came, looked at the child, and said, "If this child is yellow, then we can erase 'the eighth day' from the Torah" (in other words, if such a perfect-looking child is yellow, there would never be a bris on the eighth day). He performed the bris himself — at noon, just as the Rosh Yeshivah had wanted — and not a moment of *seder* was lost.

At the same time, the Rosh Yeshivah was a very happy, relaxed person, not in any way uptight about time. Life was meaningful, and therefore happy. Life was meant to be utilized to its fullest, and it was.

One last story, which was told by the Rebbetzin, *a"h*, upon their return over 40 years ago from the United States. The purpose of telling this now-famous story is not to make the reader say "Wow!" but to impress how much the sincere desire of a person can cause great and, yes, supernatural things to happen.

The Rosh Yeshivah was seated in front of the screen on one of his international flights. He told the flight attendant that he couldn't be seated there, right in front of the movie. She politely told him that the flight was full and there was no option to change his seat. The Rosh Yeshivah asked again and was rebuffed again.

What happened next was unbelievable. The demonstration video, which at that time used to be shown before takeoff, didn't work. Those unschooled in airplane protocol may not know that if there is any malfunction on the airplane, even if it is not life threatening, the plane will not take off.

After a short while, when attempts to air the video were for naught, the flight attendant said, "Maybe it's the rabbi." She changed his seat and, lo and behold, the video worked!

The Rosh Yeshivah would not want this story retold unless there was a purpose behind it. That purpose, I believe, is to impress upon us how far a deep desire can take us.

This was his constant message to us. He didn't grow up with any advantages. He wasn't an unbelievable genius, he didn't have a rosh yeshivah father, and his youth was not spent in an environment or city steeped in a pure Torah atmosphere. He grew up in the Lower East Side of New York City, as did so many other Jews of that generation. He even said that he was known as "Lefty" Scheinberg, because he threw a baseball with his left hand. All he had was an indomitable spirit and strong commitment and burning love for Torah. We can do it, too, he would tell us. He was a big *mechayeiv*; he made us all responsible for our growth and dedication to Torah, and he was a deep, genuine, living inspiration.

His *talmidim* will never forget his lifesaving and life-giving effect on their lives.

תהי נפשו צרורה בצרור החיים.

An expression of gratitude

It was impossible for me to write this book. The time necessary to write, which requires not only many hours, but quality, focused time as well, is simply not there. A dear friend, a noted world-class educator and writer, decided to collect some of the *shiurim* I had given and put them into writing. It took years for me to add stories and exercises for implementing the ideas expressed in the various mind-sets, but at last the minutes added up and the book was completed. I hope that people will gain from what is written here.

This friend, who also wrote the introductions to each mind-set, insisted on anonymity, and I agreed, reluctantly at first. Then I realized that he was right. Rav Elazar Menachem Mann Shach, *zt"l*, once said that when you receive honor for something, the good deed becomes like an "*oisegeklapta karta*," a bus ticket with holes punched out to record the rides already taken. When all the rides on the card have been used, it becomes nothing more than a worthless piece of paper.[2]

I wish to honor my friend and express my gratitude, but he is within his rights to refuse to have his name publicly mentioned. Still, I must say to him, "Thank you. Thank you for this book, thank you for being a good friend, and may we know each other for many more healthy, productive years."

---

2. If, however, the good deed is made known in order to inspire others, the situation is different and it can be publicized. But even then, it's better to leave at least part of the mitzvah concealed from public view. See Sfas Emes, *Terumah* 5634, s.v. "*harotzeh.*"

Mrs. Miriam Zakon, whom I have known for many years, has taken this book under skilled and sensitive wings and saw to it that it would receive the best editorial care. I applaud her choice of Mrs. Suri Brand, who has not only exhibited excellent editorial skills, but a lot of insight into how this book can better accomplish its goal of helping people better utilize their lives for growing in their *avodas Hashem*.

It's truly a privilege to have the expert hand of ArtScroll shepherd this work through to its final form. For many years I have been telling audiences that I got my definition of *professional* from Rabbi Meir Zlotowitz. Years ago I had been asked by an author, who didn't know English, to review his editor's work. It was a fine job, but there were some kinks that needed ironing out. The more issues I found, the more Rav Meir loved me. There was no defensiveness, just true joy and enthusiasm at making sure that he produced the best possible book that would be of benefit to his readership.

On a personal level, I am indebted to the *Ribbono shel Olam* for more things than I can ever enumerate. I have had the privilege to have been exposed to and held close by three life-changing mentors: Mori VeRabi HaGaon Rav Simcha Wasserman *zt'l*, Mori VeRabi HaGaon Rosh Hayeshivah Rav Chaim Pinchus Scheinberg *zt'l*, and Mori VeRabi the Mashgiach of Mirrer Yeshiva in Brooklyn, HaGaon Rav Hirsh Feldman *zt'l*. They are sorely missed and I hope that the investment that they placed in me will bear fruit that will give them *nachas* in *Olamos HaElyonim* (the Heavenly spheres).

This year Klal Yisrael sustained a terrible loss with the passing of HaGaon Rav Shlomo Brevda *zt'l*. I sat by him, as a student before his Rebbe, for five years. In that time he gave me an appreciation for the writings of the GRA and a powerful approach to understanding life. He was the epitome of a *talmid* himself; when he spoke of the Brisker Rav *zt'l* or Rav Chatzkel Levenstein *zt'l* or the Chazon Ish *zt'l* there was a palpable change in him; it was as if the Rebbe was before him. The impression he left on me was very deep. For close to 30 years he was a true inspiration to me. His loss is sorely felt by his *talmidim* and anyone who merited listening to him.

I cannot ever begin to adequately thank Hashem for my two families, those of my parents and those of my in-laws. They deserve a detailed appreciation, for honoring parents and expressing gratitude to them really has no limits.

My parents, *aleihem ha'shalom*, were and are an example to me through life, despite the many years that have elapsed since their passing. My father *a"h,* זעליג בן נח יהודה, imbued in me a deep love of learning, and the firm resolve to never stop learning throughout life .He also was a powerful symbol of integrity and all of his children and grandchildren would never consider being untruthful or dishonest, because this deeply held life principle was so ingrained in them. My mother *a"h,* אסתר בת יהושע אפרים, was *moser nefesh* for Torah her entire life, beginning with the time when, as a single person in the 1930s, she sent part of her small earnings to help sustain her brother Rav Moshe *zt'l,* who was learning in Kaminetz under the tutelage of Rav Baruch Ber *zt'l* until literally the last boat out of Europe in 1939.[3]

My father-in-law, Rabbi Solomon Freilich *shlita*, was Rav of Congregation Sons of Israel in Mount Vernon, New York for 57 years. He guided his *kehillah* with sensitivity and skill until his retirement in Eretz Yisrael. He was close with his Rebbe, Rav Yitzchok Hutner *zt'l*, retaining close contact with him from the 1940s until the Rosh Yeshivah's passing. He has always treated me as a son, and has been, for my wife and myself, a model of

---

3. My maternal grandfather owned the first *shomer Shabbos* store on 16th Avenue in Boro Park a hundred years ago. The family lived above the store, and my uncle, Rav Moshe Levy *zt'l*, told us that when customers of my grandfather's tailor shop would knock on the apartment door on Friday nights to collect their clothing, his father, my grandfather, would not answer the door. When Moshe said to his father, "*Tatteh, zei klappen*" ("Father, they are knocking"), my grandfather would say, "*Ich hehr nisht*" ("I can't hear"); he was selectively deaf to people wanting to cause him to desecrate the Shabbos.

what a parent should be. In 42 years of marriage, I have never heard anything negative from him about anyone, and he has regaled me with beautiful *divrei Torah*. His *simchas chayim* is a model for us, as he retains an optimism even through the great challenges of his life.

My mother-in-law *a"h*, אסתר בת ישראל יצחק, who passed away on 22 Cheshvan 5732, is sorely missed. She was herself a woman who was dedicated to learning, and for several decades, in the early morning hours of the day, collected and collated various commentaries on every *pasuk* of the entire Tehillim. Nevertheless, she dedicated herself totally and selflessly to her husband's work in Rabbanus and *kiruv rechokim*. Her three children are all totally and tirelessly dedicated to giving to Klal Yisrael, a testimony to her and *yb"l* her husband's joyful giving to others with an open heart and an understanding mind.

May they see *nachas* from their children, myself being one of them.

Last and most specially, my wife, Rena, is a gift from Hashem and I pray that we see continued *nachas* from our children.

About this book

There is a general life principle: the more control you have over something, the more responsibility you have for it. *There is nothing more in your control than what is going on in your head.* Therefore, you are most responsible for the mind-sets that you carry with you. Rav Mattisyahu Salomon, *shlita*, put it this way: "You are not responsible for the thoughts that come into your mind, but you are responsible for what you do with them." This is an ingenious way of expressing this idea: we can't always control our environment, but we can control our own head space.

The mind-sets selected here represent some important ways of approaching some of life's most vital and challenging areas of life.

Each mind-set concludes with a "Turning Ideas into Action" section. The inspiration, and the philosophy, behind this section was Rav Avigdor Miller, *zt"l*, who was my *mashgiach* in Yeshivas Rabbeinu Chaim Berlin. He was a genius at translating ideas into specific exercises. He maintained that these actions should be relatively small, but that they be consistent. Many beautiful examples of these exercises can be found in *Sha'arei Orah*, volumes 1 and 2, where he deals with vital subjects followed by such exercises.

In time, I learned that choosing a proper exercise entails four elements:

1. It should be a specific act and
2. a relatively easy one, to ensure continuity.

3. It should be something that I really should be doing anyway, to avoid any feelings of arrogance that I may entertain because "I'm working on myself." Arrogance from a program of self-improvement is at the very least self-defeating. Haughtiness is a terminal disease; Hashem doesn't like arrogant people. And, finally,

4. it should be an act that is directly related to the area that I am trying to improve.

The actions in this book aim to fulfill these four criteria and will help you internalize the mind-sets presented here.

A note to the reader

Whenever the words "Mori V'Rabi, *zt"l*," appear, they refer to Mori V'Rabi HaGaon HaRav Simcha Wasserman, *zt"l*.

Whenever the words "the Rosh Yeshivah, *zt"l*" appear, they refer to Mori V'Rabi HaGaon HaRav Chaim Pinchus Scheinberg, *zt"l*.

CHAPTER 1

The Happiness Mind-Set

Happiness: It's Not Easy!

eople in the Western world are enjoying health and prosperity at a level never before experienced by man. Many of us have comforts that not so long ago were accessible only to a small class of the wealthiest and most privileged. Our life spans are longer, and entertainment and knowledge are available literally at the touch of a button or the click of a mouse. So why do many people suffer from neuroses, anxieties, and psychoses? Why are antidepressants so widely prescribed and used? Why is our world gripped with such great unhappiness? More important, where can people find the happiness that seems to escape them?

The hard way

Imagine two people standing on the peak of a high mountain. One arrived there in a helicopter and took only 15 leisurely minutes to reach the top. The other person climbed up, taking three long, hard days of effort. Who has a greater sense of accomplishment?

The one who climbed the mountain clearly feels a greater sense of happiness and accomplishment than the one who did it the easy way.

We live in a time when the emphasis is on making everything easy. *The unwillingness to do anything that's hard destroys our ability to take pleasure in our achievements.* Buying into the instant, quick-fix values of Western society is a formula for unhappiness. Indeed, it is the nature of a person to find satisfaction from something that came the hard way. Human beings appreciate and savor that which they have worked for.

Superficiality: The test of our generation

I heard from Rav Avigdor Miller, *zt"l*, that one of the facets of our exile, *Galus Edom*, is that all that matters is how something looks. As someone who has been in the world of publishing, I can tell you: people judge a book by its cover. The right cover is vital. There is an entire science on what colors and fonts have what kind of suggestive effect. Political parties and advertising agencies spend millions researching these effects.

Because of this emphasis on the superficial, we are unwilling to invest in hard work. We can't keep any diet or regimen that takes a long time, because we can't see immediate results. This is why we are a depressed generation. We are not used to working hard, and so we don't taste the happiness that comes with achieving difficult things.

The "big" value of small steps

The feeling of self-worth that accompanies achievement comes *only* when we do things that are hard for us. In other words, we have to earn it. "Hard" can mean something that's difficult to accomplish, or it can mean doing something that takes a long time before we see results.[1]

But people are naturally impatient and want to see quick results from their efforts. How do we find the strength to persevere when faced with challenges that take a long time to come to successful fruition?

The key is to *appreciate and take encouragement from small steps and small accomplishments.* In this way, we gain the patience to persevere and, ultimately, to accomplish great things and experience the happiness that comes from such accomplishments.

Celebrating small victories is not always easy. The ability to be encouraged by small steps can often be the hardest thing of all to achieve. By nature, we revel in big accomplishments. The ability to value "small" accomplishments is, however, the recipe for happiness.

> Rav Moshe Aharon Shochotowitz, *shlita*, of Jerusalem relates that when he was a young child, his father brought him to the great *mashgiach* of the Ner Israel Yeshivah in Baltimore, Rav Dovid Kronglas, *zt"l*. Rav Dovid wanted to teach little Moshe Aharon a life lesson. He said to him, "*Kleine menschen machen groise zachen; groise menschen machen kleine zachen* — Small people are only willing to do 'big' things, while truly 'big' people can, and want, to do 'small' things." For in truth there are no really small or meaningless things in life. Rav Dovid had young Moshe Aharon repeat his words to instill in him a lifelong appreciation for "small" things.

About the yetzer hara

The direct connection between effort and happiness is the underlying principle behind some puzzling statements in

---

1. See *Beis HaLevi, Bereishis,* s.v. "*isa b'Midrash.*"

Chazal. The Midrash says[2] about the *pasuk* "G-d saw all that He had made, and behold it was very good"[3] that the words *tov me'od*, "very good," refer to the *yetzer hara*, the evil inclination. How can the Midrash claim that our *yetzer hara*, which gives us so much grief and trouble, is *tov me'od*, "very good"?

The answer is that if effort leads to happiness and the sense of self-worth that Hashem wants us to have, then the evil inclination is indeed a great gift, because it brings meaning and satisfaction to our lives. We work hard and confront it on so many levels, and then our achievements in overcoming it are indeed sweet.

About the road to becoming a righteous person

What does it mean when it says in *Tehillim*, "*Rabbos ra'os tzaddik* — Many are the mishaps of the righteous"[4] — that the righteous need to endure many evils on the way to being a *tzaddik*? Why is it necessary for the *tzaddik* to go through such trouble?

Similarly, the Midrash teaches that "*tzaddikim techilasan yesurim* — a *tzaddik* begins with suffering."[5] Why?

In the light of what we now know about happiness, the answers to these questions are obvious. The *tzaddik* must of necessity go through much evil, through many difficult trials, and his way must, at the beginning, be painful. He must fight and conquer much opposition on his path to righteousness. And in the end, the *tzaddik's* worth is measured by what he worked to achieve, and so is the satisfaction and happiness that he feels when he does, indeed, reach his goals.[6]

---

2. *Bereishis Rabbah* 9:7.

3. *Bereishis* 1:31.

4. *Tehillim* 34:20.

5. *Bereishis Rabbah* 2:10.

6. The Alter of Kelm, *Chochmah U'Mussar*, vol. 2, *ma'amar* 28.

In the yeshivah where I serve as *mashgiach*, there was a boy who was not particularly successful in his Torah studies. One day he decided he was going to learn, by heart, the give-and-take of one page of Gemara. He would also make the effort to understand the meaning of every word on the page and not just memorize the words.[7] It took him a long time, but when he was finished, the happiness and excitement he felt from his success has carried him to this day. Years later, he is an outstanding *masmid* who has dedicated his life to Torah. Another boy in the yeshivah gave a Torah presentation to his class after weeks of industrious preparation. He, too, felt a huge boost and great pleasure in his accomplishment.

---

7. Memorizing every word of a page of Gemara is not something I would normally recommend. For most people, this can become a burden and ruin their desire to learn. Knowing every word on the page should be the natural result of the happy review, many times over, of the page.

Turning Ideas into Action ▶

▶ *Don't put it off any longer.*

We all have things we put off because although we realize their importance, we shy away from the difficulty involved in doing them, emotionally or otherwise. Sometimes it's a long-delayed phone call, either to thank someone for something or to update a friend on good news. Sometimes it can be even harder: calling someone to ask for forgiveness.[8] When we finally make the call, we may be embarrassed at our tardiness, but the good feeling that comes from doing it serves as an impetus to continue to do things that may initially be difficult. If you've been putting it off, do it now.

▶ *Review it one more time.*

The Steipler Gaon, *zt"l*, said that when a person puts in extra effort to review the Torah that he already knows, this effort atones for sins. I would like to apply this and recommend that you review *one more time* even though you think you know the Torah that you have just learned. Here is a perfect example of what we are speaking about: accomplishing something in small steps without stressing yourself out too much.

---

8. A *rav* may have to be consulted on the right way to approach such a sensitive issue.

Connecting to Happiness

*W*e *all want to be happy. But what, exactly, does that mean?*

The elements of happiness

Things that are important have three salient characteristics:

1. They are available to all who seek them, because Hashem would never withhold something that is truly important from His creations.

2. The more vital they are, the more the *yetzer hara* will prevent us from acquiring them.

3. It takes work to achieve them.

These three characteristics apply to a tremendously sought-after and very important commodity: happiness.

Simchah, happiness, is available to all who seek it. *Happiness is everywhere.* And there are innumerable opportunities to acquire it.

Because the benefits of happiness are so great, so are the obstacles that the *sitra achra*[9] will place in the path of someone who seeks happiness. As my *mashgiach*, Rav Hirsh Feldman, *zt"l, mashgiach* of the Mirrer Yeshivah in Brooklyn, used to say, the more important something is, the greater the opposition the *yetzer hara* will offer to combat it.

And it takes work, a lot of work, to achieve true happiness.

Happiness, defined

So we know that happiness is achievable, but must be earned and fought for. But what, exactly, is happiness?

First, we must understand what happiness is not. *Happiness is not a life goal; it is an asset.* In order to be able to have the energy and staying power necessary to do important and difficult things, we need to be happy. Happiness gives us energy; Rav Avigdor Miller, *zt"l*, called happiness "high-octane fuel." The happiness that we derive from hard work and accomplishment goes on to fuel even more hard work — and more accomplishment! We don't "pursue happiness" for its own sake, but for what.it can give us: the energy and encouragement to accomplish even more.

The Maharal says[10] that true happiness stems from the realization that we are connected to Hashem. Hashem is the only thing in creation that is permanent. And the more permanent something is, the more we can derive joy from it. Nothing is more permanent, and hence joyful, than being connected to the permanent Source of everything, Hashem. In fact, there can't be absolute joy in anything physical, since the temporary nature of physical things mitigates the degree of *simchah*

---

9. Literally, "the other side"; the forces of evil that Hashem has created to oppose us in our quest for fulfilling our function in this world and serving Him, thereby giving us opportunities for growth and increased reward.

10. *Nesivos Olam, Nesiv HaTorah*, Ch. 18.

a person can have.[11] As exciting as it is to acquire new things, inevitably the thrill wears off because we become used to them and they are of a temporary nature. But when we pursue our connection to Hashem, there we can find true joy, because the happiness we derive in being close to Hashem doesn't fade.

Mori V'Rabi, *zt"l*, said that happiness is related to our ability to recognize and actualize our function, to know our purpose in life and to achieve it.

Happiness is vital

How important is this happiness? *Mesilas Yesharim*[12] teaches us that we were created to have pleasure.[13] Man seeks the pleasure of happiness more than anything else. The *true* happiness that we all instinctively seek, as just mentioned, is achieved by strengthening our connection to Hashem. That is our function and our purpose. *And achieving our purpose makes us happy.*

> I heard from Rav Avigdor Miller, *zt"l*, that Jonas Salk's wife said her husband used to come home with his lunch uneaten. He was so wrapped up in finding a cure for the dreaded disease of polio (which he ultimately achieved) that he didn't realize he was hungry. When people are engaged in meaningful activity, it not only overshadows even the most basic physical needs, but it makes them happy.

The closer our connection is to Heaven, the greater the possibility of happiness. And in the end, our connection to Hashem will be measured by the intrinsic meaningfulness of our lives: whether we lived in this world in accordance with His eternal will.

---

11. See the Alter of Kelm, *Chochmah U'Mussar*, vol. 2, *ma'amar* 161.
12. Chapter 1.
13. Even in this world — see Rav Avigdor Miller, *Sha'arei Orah*, vol. 1, p. 177.

▶ *Smile and make someone's day.*

Once a day, do something simply because it's the right thing to do and it is Hashem's will. It should be something small. Rav Avigdor Miller, *zt"l*, encouraged people to smile at someone and wish him a good day — and mean it. Our Sages taught us that Hashem bestows wondrous blessings on those who gladden the hearts of others.[14]

▶ *Say at least one of the birchos hashachar with real kavanah.*

One of the main ways we feel connected to Hashem and enjoy the happiness this brings us is through gratitude. We should feel grateful for even one of the physical and emotional gifts that we have, even if many others share these gifts. When we say even one of the morning blessings with real *kavanah*, when we thank Hashem for the ability to think, to see, to walk, for our clothing and our shoes — and everything else that we mention in the morning blessings — we will, at that moment, feel connected to Him.

---

14. *Bava Basra* 9b.

Half Full: Focusing on Our Blessings

*W*e are a generation that has benefited from immense good fortune. Spiritually it's easier to study Torah and be free to pursue the mitzvos than it has been for centuries. Physically we enjoy comforts undreamed of until recently. At the same time, the divorce rate is up, and mental health professionals have no trouble keeping busy. Our lives are filled with material prosperity and spiritual delights, yet mixed in with all the good is chronic frustration and bouts of unhappiness. We can't always control whether we will experience hardship, but we can choose our response. How can we learn to look at the glass as half full rather than half empty?

The greatest gift

Something happened to me on a trip that gave me the greatest of all gifts: a greater understanding of myself.

My plane arrived late in Toronto's Pearson Airport. I was told that I might not make my connecting flight, and for sure my bags wouldn't unless I brought them to check-in myself. I grabbed my suitcases and raced to a bus stop, where I waited for 10 minutes in the frigid Canadian air for the shuttle to Terminal 2 to arrive. I got there as the flight was boarding, and they rushed me through customs and immigration. I made the flight with barely minutes to spare. After I was seated and I'd breathed a sigh of relief that I had made the flight, bags and all, I realized that I had neglected to input my frequent flyer miles in the ticket. I could no longer do it easily, and I was upset.

Suddenly I realized that while I was busy focusing on a few lost frequent flyer miles, I had failed to see all the kindness that had just been showered on me. I had the strength and health to enable me to schlep my bags by myself; I was sitting, safe and comfortable, in the flight that I'd wanted to make.

The lesson I learned? *We are used to not noticing what's right about our lives and often overlook all that's gone well.*

Why is it so hard for us to notice the good? To understand why, let's look at the phenomenon of firsts.

The pleasure of "firsts"

Rav Moshe Feinstein, *zt"l,* says[15] that the reason we give the first fruits to the *Kohen* is to show how precious the mitzvos are to us. Rav Moshe explains that the *Kohen* sees no difference in whether he gets the first fruits or later ones; after all, a piece of fruit is a piece of fruit, no matter when it's been picked. But

---

15. *Darash Moshe, Bereishis,* p. 1, s.v. *"bereishis bara."*

for the Jew giving the fruits, there is a huge difference: the first fruits are the tangible results of an entire season of labor. Giving away something that's precious signals a love for the mitzvah, and the first fruits are the most precious of the crop.

Similarly, the first city to be conquered in Eretz Yisrael, Yericho, was dedicated to Hashem; it had a special place in our hearts, because it was the first.[16]

Why "firsts" make us happy

There are two reasons that "firsts" give us special joy:

1. We begin to see the fruits of our labor.

2. When something is brand new, we are not used to it, and therefore it is still precious to us. Later, when we have become used to the blessing, it gives us much less pleasure.

If we get used to good fortune, it no longer brings us pleasure, and then we stop focusing on what's right in our lives. This is a great source of unhappiness.

In our spiritual world, if we no longer find joy in mitzvah observance, it's because we fail to feel the pleasure of the newness of the mitzvos. They are no longer our *bikkurim,* our "first fruits." If we could hold on to the newness, we would see the wondrous kindness that surrounds us, and the mitzvos would be beloved to us. Then we would be able to give the first of everything to its rightful Owner and focus on the blessings, on the cup that's half full, paying no attention to the part that's half empty.

Notice the details

Here is an effective way to maintain a feeling of freshness for the gifts that we would otherwise fail to appreciate:

---

16. Heard from Rav Shlomo Brevda, *zt"l.*

Rav Avigdor Miller, *zt"l*, told us to look at a simple food on our plates, such as peas, and imagine all the people and work that were needed to get those peas to your plate. I recommend that young married men focus on the coffee their wives prepare for them. They give their husbands exactly the amount of coffee they like, the correct amount of sugar, the correct amount of milk — not to mention boiling the water and washing out the cup!

To retain the joy, retain the newness. To retain the newness, keep your eyes open.

Turning Ideas into Action ▶

▶ *Be conscious and conscientious.*

Once a day, before doing a mitzvah that is part of your daily routine, stop and put the action on "manual"; that is, decide to do the mitzvah and stay aware of what you are doing. All that time that you are doing that one mitzvah, don't let it go on "autopilot."

▶ *Make a mitzvah precious again.*

Take a "routine" mitzvah, such as taking challah from a batch of dough or lighting Shabbos candles, and take the time to learn about it. Then take a few minutes to learn what the mitzvah means and what it teaches us. Try to understand it better and appreciate the gift of the connection to Hashem that it gives you. For instance, study one of the *berachos* of *Shemoneh Esrei*. Distill the ideas that you learn into a better understanding of the *berachah*, or focus on the deeper meaning of some of the words contained in the *berachah*. For example, the word *chonein* in the *berachah* of *Atah Chonein*, where we request that Hashem grant us wisdom, refers to an unearned gift, freely bestowed on us by our Creator. When we realize that our ability to think, and think well, is a gift, it helps us avoid the arrogance that can come with intelligence.

▶ **Remember:** *The ideas you study should be short, easy to understand, and pertinent.*

Avoid taking on things that are a burden; you want to be able keep these actions up, at least for a defined period of time. The benefits of these exercises lie in the repetition and consistency of the act, not in any big, momentary inspiration. Keep this idea in mind when you study the mitzvah or *berachah* you have chosen to focus on for an extended period of time, such as a month or more — for as long as it inspires you or until it becomes part of your natural, effortless understanding of the mitzvah. Then you can move on to study another mitzvah or *berachah*.

Finding Meaning and Joy Through the Seder

*W*e know that the Seder experience is fundamental to in-
culcating us with faith in the Creator and transmitting
Judaism to the next generation. Seder night can also
teach us to attain — and hopefully retain — a joyous mind-set.

Three ways to happiness

Rav Mattisyahu Salomon, *shlita*, quoting from Rav Chaim
Vital's *Sefer HaKedushah*, teaches that we can achieve joy in
three ways:

1. Know that "*kol avid Rachmana l'tav avid* — everything that
Hashem does is for good."

2. One should "motivate himself to achieve the epitome
of joy in the service of his Creator." As we mentioned before
(Mind-Set 2), joy comes from being connected to Hashem.

3. "Make your Torah your set occupation and your mundane work happenstance." Emphasize Torah — that is, the spiritual part of life — over the material aspects and you will achieve joy.

The common denominator of these three elements is that they all emphasize the fact that *our lives have meaning*. Since there is a God, and since everything He does is good for us, then everything that happens to us happens for a reason and nothing, no event, is meaningless.

Meaning = joy

There is a clear and strong connection between joy and meaning. Even difficult things are not a burden when they are meaningful. The worst part of the Egyptian torture was the meaninglessness of the work: the Jewish people were forced to build storehouses in places where they knew the structures would collapse.

In the early 20th century, this punishment took the form of giving a convict in prison a heavy sledgehammer and ordering him to produce 50 pounds of rock dust by the end of the day. If the rock dust would have been used for something that mattered, the punishment would have consisted only of the hard physical labor. The worst part of the punishment was the convict's knowledge that after all his backbreaking labor, the rock dust would be tossed into the river.

When we know that things that happen to us have a purpose, we can feel *simchah* in those things, even (or perhaps especially) if things are hard. Despair comes when someone goes through a difficult experience and feels it was for nothing, that there was no purpose to his suffering.

The Sfas Emes says[17] that the main thing that a person wants to know about life is what he was created for. People search for joy and therefore they search for meaning.

---

17. *Bamidbar*, p. 16, s.v. *"b'Midrash heviani."*

The elements of joy in the Seder

These three elements of joy can all be found at the Seder:

1. *"Everything that Hashem does is for good."* It says of the Seder, *"Maschilim bigenus u'mesayemim b'shevach — We begin with a description of our disgrace and end with praise."*[18] When we look back, we see the goodness even in the harsh decrees, that all that Hashem did was for good. We realize that the harshness prepared us to handle everything we would have to confront. We realize that everything — even suffering — has meaning, and this brings us joy.

2. One should *"motivate himself to achieve the epitome of joy in the service of His Creator."* The obligation to mention the *korban Pesach*, matzah, and *maror*[19] represents the service of Hashem. The fact that they are commandments from God shows that we changed our status from being servants of Pharaoh to being servants of Hashem. The commandments connect us to Hashem because only when I do something simply because Hashem commanded it am I really connected to Him.

This is what we mean when we say in our blessings, *"asher kideshanu b'mitzvosav — Who has sanctified us with His commandments"*: that we are in צוותא (from the same root as the word מצוות), in "company" with Hashem, when we do His commandments. This connection is a source of joy to us, because it imbues all our actions with meaning.

3. *"Make your Torah your set occupation and your mundane work happenstance."* I once heard Rav Mattisyahu Salomon, *shlita*, say that we endured the servitude of Egypt in order to be able to understand the essence of a servant's life. A slave has no place in this world; he exists only for the sake of his master. For him, everything physical in this world is temporary, depending totally on his master's whim. His spirituality, on the

---

18. *Pesachim* 116a.
19. Ibid.

other hand, is truly his, and no master can deprive him of it. It is in the permanence of spirituality that he can find meaning and joy.

Since we are servants of Hashem, *everything* we do in His service has meaning; it is our spiritual lives that will last eternally and that will therefore be our source of true happiness.

On Seder night we celebrate leaving the bondage of Pharaoh, which rendered our lives meaningless, to begin a new life of meaning, and therefore a life of true joy.

I remember being with my father in Beth Israel Hospital in New York in 1996. I turned off his phone since the calls were all for me and the ring sometimes woke him. On the opposite side of the room lay a Mr. Singer, who offered to take calls for me. When I said to him, "Mr. Singer, you're not well. Why should I bother you with this?" he replied, "I want to do something for someone." Mr. Singer, as ill and weak as he was, still sought meaning in his life, and therefore joy. To him that meant being a giver, being able to mean something to someone. In this way, he could remain loyal to his true identity as a person created in the image of God, the ultimate Giver. This was his connection to Hashem in which he found joy.

Another time, a dear friend of mine was hospitalized with terminal stomach cancer. The doctors told him he had only a short time to live, and people were coming to his bedside to say good-bye to him. He told me 20 years later (in the end he was cured and is well to this day, thank G-d) that someone came to him and said that a young man and a young woman would be visiting him separately. This person felt that the two would be a good match and asked my friend to suggest the *shidduch* during their visits. "At first I thought that the person suggesting this was crazy," my friend said, "but then I realized that he had been my best visitor, because he had given me a function. I could still do something for someone."

Turning Ideas into Action ▶

▶ *Take stock.*

Before saying the *berachah "shelo asani aved* — that
You did not make me a slave" in the morning, realize
that slaves have no meaning in their lives; they are only
adjuncts of their master, who could easily condemn
them to a life of backbreaking work in order to make
a tiny profit. What a joy it is to have a life of meaning,
to be able to build your own future, in this world and
the next!

▶ *Appreciate that you are a servant of Hashem and not a
slave to a human master.*

Reflect, before doing any mitzvah, on the fact that a
human master is concerned only with his own benefit, not the benefit of his slaves. Hashem, on the other
hand, commands us to do mitzvos for our benefit, not
His.

▶ *Think of others.*

Think about the people in your life to whom you mean
something. Thank Hashem for these relationships, for
the meaning they bring to *your* life. Think about what
you could do, in some small way, to keep that relationship healthy. And think about people with whom you
can build a relationship. Consider becoming a "big

brother" or "big sister" to a person who needs someone like that in his life. I've often told students returning to their home country after a year or two in Israel, where they underwent huge, positive changes, to meet with their high school principal and offer to help a student in the school who could benefit from such a relationship.

CHAPTER 2

Being the Best We Can Be

The Path to the Next World: Character Traits

*F*rom our perspective, they are seemingly harmless: those critical, caustic, or witty comments about others. Heaven's perspective is a bit different.

Hashem is the true Judge

Rav Yitzchak Hutner, *zt"l*, taught that the difference between the heavenly court and the earthly court is that the earthly court has no right to judge a person.[1] The judges of *beis din* are only emissaries of Hashem: "*ki hamishpat l'Elokim hu* — justice belongs only to Hashem."[2] The court has the right to judge the *act*, but not the *person*.

---

1. *Pachad Yitzchak*, Shavuos, *ma'amar* 44.
2. *Devarim* 1:17.

Once a person has been convicted, the earthly court does not have permission to forgive. It is only empowered to evaluate whether or not the act was committed, not whether or not the perpetrator is a good person.

The heavenly court, on the other hand, can determine whether the person is good or bad. Therefore the heavenly court can also forgive the person if it sees that he has changed. In short, the heavenly court takes the person's *character*, not just the action, into consideration. *It is the character traits of a person, much more than his actions, that reflect the essence of the individual.*

The root of all evil

We are taught that publicly embarrassing someone is worse than murder. In fact, a person loses his portion in the Next World for such an action.[3] This well-known principle is difficult to understand. How can shaming someone be worse than killing him? After all, when a person embarrasses another, the culprit can still do *teshuvah*, but a murderer can't bring his victim back to life.

When we realize that the heavenly court takes character into consideration, this principle isn't so perplexing. It's true that in a human court the sin of murder, which is a capital crime, is worse than the sin of denigrating someone, but embarrassing another person is rooted in the negative *middah* (character trait) of mocking that which has value. Someone who habitually denigrates others lacks the ability to appreciate things and that will carry over to not appreciating the *Shechinah*, the Divine Presence. Once someone does not see worth in Hashem's

---

3. See Rabbeinu Yonah on *Avos* 3:11. There is actually a discussion among halachic authorities whether one is obligated to give up his life rather than embarrass someone, just as one is obligated to give up his life rather than murder someone. See also Avrohom Tobolsky, *Hizaharu Bichvod Chavreichem* (Bnei Brak, 1981), p. 123.

gifts, he has no compunction violating Hashem's commands. Therefore, for the act of embarrassing another, which is rooted in bad *middos* and can lead to transgressions, the heavenly court takes away a person's portion in the Next World.

> Someone came to the Chasam Sofer to be tested for acceptance into the yeshivah in Pressburg for the winter term. Although the candidate did well on the test, the Chasam Sofer refused to admit him into the yeshivah. When asked why, he said that as he and the young man walked to the Chasam Sofer's home, they passed some *s'chach* that someone had obviously discarded after the recent Succos holiday. The young man stepped on the *s'chach*, making no effort to avoid it. "Someone who can tread on something that had so recently been used for a mitzvah I cannot accept into my yeshivah," the Chasam Sofer declared.

For this reason, Rav Tzadok HaKohen of Lublin said[4] that *leitzanus*, mockery, is the root of all evil, for the source of all evil is denigrating that which has value. Similarly, no sin, says Rav Yerucham Levovitz,[5] is as serious as despising that which has value, for it reveals a gaping hole in the person's soul.

Negative character traits are worse than the sin

We see that sometimes what seems to be a "small" sin is actually representative of something much worse. It represents some deep, tragic flaw in a person. In fact, Chazal viewed a negative *middah* as very, very serious. For example, they teach us that someone who gets angry will be subject to many forms

---

4. *Tzidkas HaTzaddik* 259.
5. *Da'as Chochmah U'Mussar*, vol. 3, *ma'amarim* 31–33.

of suffering in Gehinnom.[6] Rav Eliyahu Lopian, *zt"l*, expressed this sharply when he said that a sin is like a counterfeit bill, and the trait that powers it is the printing press.[7]

> When the Chafetz Chaim heard that a student was about to be ejected from the yeshivah for desecrating Shabbos, he asked to speak to the young man and succeeded in getting him to change his ways. On the other hand, when he heard that a boy had been rude and brazen to someone who cooked for the yeshivah, he ordered the boy sent away.

Appreciating others

If negative traits can be damaging, positive character traits can result in enormous rewards, including the greatest of them: *Olam Haba*, the Next World.

The underlying trait that paves our path to the Next World is appreciating the value of others. The Gemara says[8] that Rabbi Eliezer specified two points that enable a person to enter *Olam Haba*:

1. Be careful with the honor of your friends.
2. Know before Whom you stand.

Rabbi Eliezer was telling his students that the path to the Next World lies in our ability to show honor, both to Hashem and to others. It doesn't matter who those others are or what their position in life is.

> The Chafetz Chaim employed a young girl to help with housework. He warned her that many guests often came through the house and there would be a lot of work. Although the girl was happy with the arrange-

---

6. *Nedarim* 22a.
7. *Lev Eliyahu*, vol. 2, *Vayechi*.
8. *Berachos* 28b.

ment because many of the visitors would leave her a tip, the Chafetz Chaim would still ask her every year, on Yom Kippur eve, to forgive him in case anything had upset her in the course of her work for him that year.

Turning Ideas into Action

▶ *See the good in others.*

Once a day, choose a person and find some positive character trait he possesses that you can admire. Focus on the same person for as long as possible so that this new understanding has a lasting effect on you. It's even better if this person is a spouse, child, or parent-in-law, since in time your appreciation of him will have a powerful positive impact on the whole family. When you truly admire and respect someone, the feeling is usually returned. As Shlomo HaMelech said, "As water reflects a face, so do the hearts of people reflect each other."[9]

▶ *Pity the bad.*

If you see someone who possesses a negative trait, feel sorry for him. This exercise will especially help you if the person causes you to suffer as a result of his poor character. You will come to realize that the person who suffers most in life is the person of poor character himself. Also, since you can feel only one emotion at a time, your feelings of pity will help you focus your emotions elsewhere. Instead of feeling anger or hatred toward that person, you will feel sorry for him.

9. *Mishlei* 27:19.

The End and the Beginning: Faith

N ext time you get a pang when you read an advertisement inviting you to spend Pesach in some exotic locale and you realize that you can't afford it...think twice before you feel deprived.

The preservative of the Ten Commandments

The Shem MiShmuel says[10] that the reason that the words *Aseres HaDibros*, "*The* Ten Commandments," are used instead of *Asarah Dibros*, "Ten Commandments," is because all the Ten Commandments are interconnected. The phrase *Aseres HaDibros* turns them into a unit.

---

10. *Shem MiShmuel, Chayei Sarah*, p. 224, in the name of the Kotzker.

How do they connect to one another?

To answer this question, we can apply an important principle to the structure of the *Aseres HaDibros*: *the function of things that come at the end is to preserve all that came before them.* For example, a witness's signature appears at the end of a document to ensure the document's validity even if the witness is no longer present.

Similarly, *Koheles* tells us that *yiras Hashem*, awe of G-d, comes at the end, because it is the preservative of all the good deeds that we perform.[11] For the same reason, the advice of the Mishnah to judge favorably appears at the end of the *mishnah* regarding making a friend and teacher.[12] This teaches us that even if you succeed in making a friend or teacher, you will not be able to keep the relationship strong unless you judge the person favorably. It is almost inevitable that people in long-term relationships will do something that we don't like; in order to preserve the relationship, we need to judge them favorably.[13]

And, as Rav Yitzchak Hutner, *zt"l*, pointed out in the name of the Gra, the last mitzvah in the Torah is the commandment to write it down: to preserve the Torah in print.[14]

In the light of this, we need to explore the significance of why "*Lo sachmod* — Do not covet" comes at the end of the Ten Commandments.

Thought, speech, and deed

To understand the structure of the Ten Commandments, we first have to recognize that man functions on three basic levels: thought, speech, and deed. Usually, man begins with

---

11. See *Koheles* 12:13.
12. *Avos* 1:6.
13. Maharal, *Derech Chaim*, on *Avos* 1:6.
14. *Sefer HaZikaron, Pachad Yitzchak*, p. 130.

thought, then proceeds to speech, and, finally, to action. This is, indeed, the order of the first five commandments, those that relate to man's relationship with G-d. We are first commanded regarding our beliefs (i.e., our thoughts), then we are forbidden to speak G-d's Name in vain (speech), and, finally, we are commanded to keep Shabbos and to honor our parents, (deeds).

On the left side of the tablets, however, where the commandments related to the relationship between man and his fellow man appear, the order is reversed. First we are commanded not to murder, commit adultery, or kidnap — all actions. Then we are told not to use our speech to swear falsely in court. Only at the end are we instructed not to covet, which is a sin committed through our thoughts.

Why is the order different on the right side of the tablets, which details sins between man and G-d, than on the left side, where sins between man and his fellow man are delineated?

One reason given is based on Rav Samson Raphael Hirsch's commentary on *Shemos*.[15] He explains that when it comes to dealings between ourselves and G-d, I might think that what matters most is what I believe followed by what I say, but does G-d really care if I switch on a light on Shabbos? So we declare that not only does G-d care about our beliefs, but also about what we say, and even what we do. In fact, we conclude these five commandments with deeds, because it is our actions that preserve the relationship between us and Hashem.

With regard to man and man, however, I might think that what matters most is what I do, less so what I say, and who cares what I think? The Torah tells us in these five commandments that Hashem does care about our thoughts when it comes to our relationships with others. Even more, it is the commandment of "*Lo sachmod* — Do not covet" that comes at the end to reveal a vital principle.

What is that vital principle?

---

15. Rav Hirsch on *Shemos* 20:14.

The truth about faith

Citing the Recanati, Rav Eliyahu Eliezer Dessler, *zt"l*, teaches that the prohibition of *lo sachmod* is based on *emunah*, faith.[16] Someone who truly has faith in G-d believes that everything he needs has been given to him — *and if he doesn't have it, he doesn't need it*. A person like that will not covet what others have.

Jealousy, coveting something that belongs to someone else, is the opposite of *emunah*. True faith includes the belief that everything Hashem gave me, or didn't give me, has a purpose.

So the Ten Commandments end the way they begin: with *emunah*. According to the Rambam,[17] the first commandment, "*Anochi Hashem* — I am your G-d," is a commandment on *emunah*. The last commandment, too, exhorts us to have *emunah*: by acknowledging that what we don't have is not for us.

This absolute faith that Hashem has provided all we need, this aspect of *emunah*, comes at the end, because it is our state of mind that guarantees the permanence of Torah observance. That is, just as the commandment of "*Anochi Hashem*," our belief in Hashem, should be primary in our minds, the feeling of "*Lo sachmod*," that we have everything we need, should be primary in our emotions. When we have these principles in mind, we will be able to serve Hashem the way we should.

Our own emotional reality

The commandment of *lo sachmod*, vital as it is, is not always simple to fulfill. How do we ensure that we don't feel jealous of others, that we don't covet what they have? How do we bring this final commandment into our own emotional reality?

There are two principles we must bear in mind:

1. *Look at the big picture.* Looking at the whole picture is a function of the intellect rather than emotion. The command-

---

16. *Michtav MeEliyahu*, vol. 1, p. 126.

17. *Sefer HaMitzvos, aseh* 1.

ment of *lo sachmod* says, "*Lo sachmod...kol asher l'rei'echa* — Do not covet...*everything* your friend has."[18] In other words, look at *everything*, at the whole picture: if you're going to be jealous of his Porsche and his designer home with the in-ground pool, are you willing to take on his ulcer also?

2. *A person who is satisfied and happy doesn't need to look elsewhere.* Rav Yitzchak Zilberstein, *shlita*, brings a beautiful parable that relates to this:[19]

> A diamond merchant on a business trip was about to re-turn home when he was offered an unbelievable deal. The only problem was, if he bought the merchandise, he would not have enough money to travel the way he was used to: first class. Since he knew it was the deal of a lifetime, he spent the money on the jewels and trav-eled coach. Whenever the journey became too hard for him, he would take out his diamonds and look at them, and he instantly felt renewed happiness, knowing that the difficulties were worth it.

So, too, the Torah Jew, who does not spend his life in pursuit of material wealth, usually can't travel first class in this world, but he looks at his diamonds — the meaningful life he lives — and he is comforted. Certainly he feels no envy or jealousy of others who have more.

When I appreciate what I have, I will not be jealous of what you have

A wonderful person once shared with me the attitude she tries to instill in her children: "Not only do I tell them that the cup is half full, I also tell them to notice that the cup itself is beautiful."

---

18. *Shemos* 20:14.

19. Chafetz Chaim, *Shem Olam, Sha'ar Hachzakas HaTorah*, Ch. 10.

Turning Ideas into Action ▶

▶ *Once a day, focus on — indeed, savor — the positive elements in your life.*

Even if there is pain and frustration, and even if the pain seems to occupy the major part of your life situation, take a few moments to see what's right in your life.

▶ *Keep a record.*

Rav Chatzkel Levenstein, *zt"l*, once advised Rav Shlomo Brevda, *zt"l*, on how people can sharpen their *emunah*: Keep a record of those things that seemed at first to be negative and in the end turned out to be positive. This is the proverbial "missing the plane that later crashed" analogy. It doesn't have to be so dramatic, though. Take, for example, some of my personal experiences:

1. I needed to see someone in the Mattesdorf section of Jerusalem about an important matter, and I had just missed the number 3 bus at the corner of Nechemia and Yechezkel Streets. It would be a 20-minute wait for the next bus or a 20-minute walk; either way I would be late. For some reason I can't remember, perhaps money, I couldn't take a cab. So I waited. When I arrived at the person's home, I was informed — mistakenly, as it turned out — that he had left for the airport. As I walked up the stairs, I met him coming

on his way down to his apartment, and we were able to talk. If I had made the bus I had wanted, I would have arrived earlier and missed an important meeting.

2. On a flight from Israel to LA with a stopover in Toronto, El Al upgraded me, putting me in business class and taking away my economy-class exit row seat. Then they mistakenly revoked my upgrade. By that time my exit row seat had been given to someone else. I was upset, since the trip to LA is a long one and I had a busy schedule to cope with as soon as I landed. I was put in the back of the plane, and when I got there I was seated next to a Jew who had "I am a *talmid chacham* and I know Hebrew" written all over him. At the time I was worried about the Hebrew translation of one of my books and had it with me on the flight. I showed it to my seatmate. He went over a large part of the book, made a few important comments, and reassured me about the translation. He turned out to be Rabbi Shlomo Gemara, *rosh yeshivah* of a high school in Toronto. He got off in Toronto — and El Al upgraded me for the rest of the flight to LA.

Being Inspired — and Staying That Way

*W**ow! We're excited, we're energized, we're inspired…and days later we're back to where we started from. How can we turn inspiration into something that will really last?*

Excitement and energy in our service of Hashem

Rav Tzadok HaKohen of Lublin says[20] that when a person begins his service of Hashem, he needs to do it with a jump start, with energy and excitement. Afterward he can introduce his intellect as a stabilizing factor.

This is analogous to the tremendous energy that a space-craft must use to break out of the bonds of the earth's gravita-

---

20. *Tzidkas HaTzaddik* 1.

tional pull; only afterward does it use its thrusters to achieve a stable orbit. First comes the *hisorerus*, the inspiration; then comes the work that makes it a permanent feature in our lives.

Inspiration internalized

The Sfas Emes says[21] that when we first left Egypt, we left in a rush, and therefore this event could not be permanent. We needed to backtrack, return to Egypt, and encamp at Baal Tzefon.[22] Then we had to leave again, this time unhurriedly, with deliberation and with forethought. Only then would our exodus become permanent and lasting. These were, according to the Sfas Emes, the two parts of the Exodus: first leaving with alacrity, "*b'chipazon,*"[23] and then going back toward Egypt, to Baal Tzefon, and doing it again, this time more slowly. *When a person goes back to apply intellect and forethought, there is permanence.*

When we grow by a sudden leap, triggered by the emotions and galvanized by some inspirational event, our growth is not yet permanent. Unless it is internalized through our efforts and determination, it will dissipate. Here are just a few examples from our history:

> There was enormous inspiration and energy created when the Red Sea split, but shortly afterward, a mere three days later, that inspiration dissipated and was replaced with complaints against Hashem and Moshe.
>
> The inspiration of *mattan Torah* (the giving of the Torah) at Har Sinai began with an enormous inspiration from Above (called "*isarusa d'le'eila*").[24] This inspiration

---

21. *Shemos* 5675, s.v. "*davar.*"
22. See *Shemos* 14:2.
23. *Devarim* 16:3.
24. See Rav Eliyahu Eliezer Dessler, *Michtav MeEliyahu*, vol. 2, p. 35.

was not a result of slow, intellectual work, and therefore it lasted only 40 days, until the sin of the golden calf. Indeed, this is why the *kedushah*, the sanctity of Har Sinai, was not permanent. In contrast, the *kedushah* of Har HaMoriah, the site of the Beis HaMikdash, is eternal. That *kedushah* was the result of a lifetime of slow and painstaking work and devotion on Avraham's part, work that ultimately led to the *akeidah* on that site, where Avraham demonstrated his willingness to sacrifice even his beloved son to Hashem.

The *kedushah* of the *Levi'im,* which they earned when they refrained from participating in the sin of the golden calf, is eternal. In contrast, the *bechoros*, the firstborn, who received their *kedushah* as a gift and never had to work to keep it, lost their *kedushah*, and their right to serve as the *Kohanim* of the nation was taken away.

Many of us know the famous statement of Chazal that Mashiach will come if the Jewish nation will keep two Shabbosos in a row.[25] Why two Shabbosos? The first Shabbos is an inspirational gift from Heaven. The second is the Shabbos that was preceded by the week's work of internalizing the *hisorerus*, the inspiration, of the first Shabbos.[26]

Where does the energy come from?

Where does a person get the energy for the initial "takeoff"? *Energy comes from the emotion, not the intellect.* This is the approach we use with our children. First and foremost we inculcate in our children the desire and ability to have an emotional

---

25. *Shabbos* 118b.
26. See *Kedushas HaShabbos, ma'amar* 2; *Shem MiShmuel, Shemos,* p. 169.

relationship with Hashem. Once they mature, the intellectual understanding and the desire to achieve that emotional connection will follow suit.

It is this emotional connection to Hashem that enables the child to do mitzvos even without prior understanding.

How to solidify an emotional advance

The Shem MiShmuel says[27] that after an emotional advance, a person should immediately learn Torah in depth. This holds true for women as well as men: although women do not have an ongoing obligation to study Torah for its own sake, they will also be able to retain their inspiration through studying topics of *emunah* and *bitachon* and by learning the deeper meaning of the *tefillos* that they say.

Once again, the beginning is an emotional one, but the preservative is intellectual, which is characterized by the in-depth study of Torah.

Energy that lasts

There is a combination of energy and stability that comes from beginning with inspiration and then preserving with introspection. This was the challenge after the Exodus, the splitting of the Red Sea, and *mattan Torah*. The people couldn't help but be inspired by those extraordinary events. But then they had to learn that when you are inspired, don't expect it to last forever, unless you take steps to preserve it.

The intellect has a memory; it can recall the past. It can also project the future: "Who is wise? One who can see what will come about."[28] Wisdom provides foresight. The emotions, on

---

27. *Acharei Mos*, p. 259.
28. *Tamid* 32a.

the other hand, know only the present. When we are inspired, it feels like our present inspiration will last forever. And it can — if we take steps to preserve it.

When we say that a wise man sees the future, we also mean that he sees the future and pulls it into his present. He can then act wisely, using his intellect to see the consequences and his emotions to give him the energy to act.[29] This is the challenge of everyone who has been inspired and elevated to highs that only emotion can reach: to take that inspiration and make it a stable part of oneself.

---

29. There is a saying: "Do as I say and not as I do." That is, do as my mind, with its wisdom, can forecast, and not as I do — not as my present-focused emotions have led me. This is a common mantra among smokers. They understand intellectually that their future will be damaged if they continue smoking, but they do it anyway because they want a cigarette *now*. If you asked a smoker if you should start smoking, however, he would advise you not to start.

Turning Ideas into Action▶

▶ *Engrave it in your memory.*

When something inspiring happens to you, or there is a moment of truth when you suddenly see the numerous gifts in your life, memorize your surroundings. Utilize all of your senses. Is it hot or cold, quiet or noisy, day or night? Who or what was around you? What did they look like? Touch something to integrate that sense into your memory. Was there a taste involved? Then, when you want to relive the inspiration or emotion, pull out the entire picture, with all of the senses involved, and the inspiration will come with it. Sometimes you can savor a quiet moment in the same way. If you are able to visit a quiet area at the beach, listen to the sounds of the sea, the smell of the ocean, the feeling of the sand. Later you can retrieve the memory and experience the same peace you felt at that moment. This idea definitely works.

MIND-SET 8

Achieving Great Things with Patience and Persistence

S *ometimes we think that if we don't push ourselves we'll never get things done, but after a while we get tired and give up. What's the right way to propel ourselves forward? What's the secret to sustaining persistence?*

Taking responsibility for ourselves

Many of us prefer not to assume responsibility. We want to be free and easy, not work so hard — especially on ourselves. Yet we must know that above all we need to take responsibility for ourselves. In the end of the day, we will be answerable to Hashem for not having used the potential that He gave us. We don't like to think about it, but it's a reality: we are responsible.

Rav Moshe Feinstein, *zt"l*,[30] and the Shem MiShmuel[31] both say that we will be reproved for not having achieved the enormous potential that is within us.

How do we achieve that potential?

The answer is twofold: patience and persistence.

The small achievements

Almost everything in life requires patience, both in Torah study and in character development. *Things worth doing or achieving generally take time.* Indeed, the fact that the accomplishment takes time to achieve increases our appreciation of it all the more when we finally reach our goal and reap the rewards of our patience.[32]

Patience is one part of the picture; the other is persistence. We need to push on and not get discouraged, even when things are hard. One way to help us keep on working, even in the face of difficulties, is to *treasure and appreciate the things we've accomplished along the way.* Taking measure of what we have already done helps us to avoid despairing over the tasks that remain before us. It is especially important to nurture and appreciate small gains, because they are the most frequent. When we allow ourselves to focus on the small achievements, we come to realize that no change or accomplishment is really small, either because it is, in itself, important or because an accumulation of "small" gains leads up to a large gain.

The great leaders of our nation never saw a necessary act as being "small."

The *gaon* Rav Yechezkel Abramsky, *zt"l*, was once walking down a street in Bayit Vegan, Jerusalem, after giving

---

30. *Derash Moshe, Vayishlach*, p. 26, s.v. "*katonti.*"

31. *Vayigash*, p. 271, s.v "*b'Midrash Rabbah.*"

32. The Sfas Emes says (*Korach* 5636, p. 113, s.v. "*v'al pi*") that we measure the greatness of a person by his ability to treasure small gains. (See also Mind-Set 28, "Elul: Small Beginnings.")

a lecture. He passed a little girl who was sitting and crying. Rav Yechezkel asked her what her name was, and she answered, "Shoshana." When he asked her why she was crying, she said that her friend had told her that her dress wasn't pretty. Rav Yechezkel, who was known to all the children on that block, said, "Go and tell your friend that the Rav said you have a pretty name and a pretty dress." The girl jumped up in joy and raced back to her friend. When Rav Yechezkel was asked why he'd stopped to address such a childish issue, he said, "We know that Hashem wipes the tears off faces.[33] We can do the same."

The true meaning of mesirus nefesh

There is a great misunderstanding about the concept of *mesirus nefesh*. People think it means forcing yourself to do things that are really hard and that run against our nature. This approach does not work in the long run: people burn out and sometimes have a hard time getting back on track.

One aspect of *mesirus nefesh* is to develop the willingness to do things that are difficult but *doable*, and to do them persistently and consistently. I often tell people, "You can walk across Russia — one step at a time." As with physical exercise, it's hard to work on ourselves continually, but ultimately the persistent and consistent work builds us up. *Ongoing, doable effort will build us, not break us.*

---

33. As it is written, "Hashem / Elokim will erase tears from all faces" (*Yeshayahu* 25:8).

Turning Ideas into Action ▶

▶ *Make small gains to complete a big project.*

Take a short *sefer* and study it for five minutes a day. Every few days, use the five minutes to review what you have done until then. After 20 pages, you may need a week to complete the review; it doesn't matter, take your time.

Choose a *sefer* that

1. is of interest to you, either because you always wanted to learn this book or it has practical relevance to your life, such as a work on guarding your tongue from improper speech;

2. is not too complicated; and

3. has natural breaks in it (numbered paragraphs, short chapters).

Pick a set time, if possible toward the beginning of the day; that way, if you miss any given morning you can make it up later. If you miss a day, don't fret about it.

It's important that it not be a difficult project. The *Sefer HaYashar* teaches us that consistency is more important than large spurts.[34] In addition, there is no need for accomplishment to equal stress; many of us have a surplus of that in our day and we don't have to add to it.

---

34. "It is better for a person to have small, but consistent, achievements, than a larger, but short-lived, accomplishment" — *Sefer HaYashar*, Gate 13.

After a month, look back and take pride and pleasure at what you have accomplished in a small amount of time. It's important to savor the pleasure; it will help you continue this and other "small" projects.

The Great Challenge: Fulfilling My Potential

So I want to be the best "I" that I can be, not comparing myself to others but still fulfilling my own potential. Remember the famous chassidic tale of the holy Reb Zishe? He taught that when his soul stood before his Creator he would not be asked why he hadn't been Moshe Rabbeinu. He would be asked only, "Zishe, why were you not Zishe?" — that is, why weren't you all that you could have been?

How, in fact, can I become the very best me?

No regrets

Rav Moshe Feinstein, *zt"l*, says[35] that everyone should be concerned that perhaps he has not actualized all that he had the potential to accomplish. This may be the harshest judgment of

---

35. *Darash Moshe, Vayishlach*, p. 26, s.v. "*katonti*."

all that we will face after 120 years: when we see what we could have achieved and compare it to what we actually did.

> The story is told of a youngster who heard his father tell his mother that he had no choice: tomorrow he would apprentice young Naftali to the tailor, since the boy wasn't showing promise in his learning. The boy, hearing those words, promised to be more diligent, and ultimately became the famed Netziv, head of the yeshivah in Volozhin. The Netziv used to say that had he become a tailor's apprentice, he would have become a good and honest tailor, a fine "*baalebos*" and a good Jew, but when he would have come to *Shamayim*, he would have been confronted with the question "Where is your *sefer Ha'amek She'eilah*?"

Yes, there is no question that a person must develop his or her potential. The question is how?

How we achieve our potential

Our potential can be achieved in two ways:

1. *Through proactive, positive activity*. We must take proactive actions to develop our ability to think, to keep our bodies strong and our minds alert.

2. *Through avoiding negative activity*. We avoid wrongdoing when we make sure that we are not affected by things that can destroy or limit our ability to grow; when we invest effort to keep negative things out of our lives and minds.

However, there are three aspects of our lives that affect our ability to accomplish:[36]

1. *Genetics*. A person should take into account his genetic reality. If he has genetically high cholesterol, he needs drugs

---

36. See Rav Yehoshua Heller, *zt"l* (1814–1880), *Divrei Yehoshua*, Ch. 1, *ma'amar* 2.

or a special diet to control it. A person with a heart condition can't live in a place located at a high altitude (Mori V'Rabi, *zt"l*, wouldn't go to Santa Fe because of its elevation), and if he has lung problems he shouldn't move to overcrowded and polluted Mexico City. People with ADD have to learn to function while taking into account their challenges. But — *no one is condemned to a failed life whatever his genetic background.*

> A *bachur* once came to Rav Moshe Aharon Shochotowitz, *shlita*, and said that he couldn't learn more than six hours a day, and even that with great difficulty. It bothered him, since the diligent students in yeshivah could study 16 hours a day. Rav Moshe Aharon immediately asked the *bachur* to give him a blessing. He said it was as if he was learning 600 hours a day, as it says, "Once in suffering is like more than 100 without suffering."[37] The *bachur* thought Rav Moshe Aharon was not being serious. They were in Bnei Brak at the time, and Rav Moshe Aharon told him to go into the home of any great man and he would see that what Rav Moshe Aharon had said was true. The *bachur* chose to visit Rav Chaim Kanievsky, *shlita*. He related everything to Rav Chaim, and Rav Chaim's response was exactly the same — "Six hundred hours a day! Please, can I have a *berachah* from you!" Today the *bachur* is a respected married man. He can still learn only six hours a day, but he is thorough, and although he is not a *lamdan*, he is known for his encyclopedic breadth of knowledge.

2. *Environment.* Our environment has a marked effect on how much we realize our potential. We need energy to fight off a negative environment, while an environment that is conducive to our spiritual growth gives us a "push" in the right direction. Though it's true that fighting a negative environment can

---

37. *Avos D'Rabbi Nassan* 3:6.

sometimes help us develop spiritual "muscles," it's not something we look for: there is always the danger of failure, and even if we succeed, we may have to use energy that we could have used to draw ourselves up higher. How much energy we need is determined by just how negative the environment is.

If through no choice of his own a person finds himself in a bad environment, he must find a handful of like-minded souls who can encourage one another to ward off the ill effect of the environment. For this to be effective, they must truly be close.

> My wife's grandfather, Reb Elozor Freilich, *zt"l*, found himself in New York City in the 1920s, a time when all too many Jews were casting off their religious observance and beliefs. He managed to ward off the ill effects of an environment that insisted that you could only succeed in America if you desecrated Shabbos by meeting with a group of friends for *melaveh malkah* every *motza'ei Shabbos*. At these gatherings, each gave the others energy to cope with the coming week, when they often had to find a new job! Out of gratitude for what he felt he'd gained from the mitzvah of *melaveh malkah*, he observed it with a *minyan* his entire life. He passed away on a *motza'ei Shabbos*, the time we eat *melaveh malkah*.

3. *Habit.* We usually function on automatic pilot, and our habits have a powerful effect on who we become. Since it's so hard to break a habit, we must develop new habits if we want to fulfill our full potential. The old ones will atrophy, while we will be busying ourselves with the good things we have habituated ourselves to do.

Who am I? What am I capable of?

These three aspects of our lives determine what is hard for us and what comes easily: our inborn nature, the environment we grew up in along with the education we received, and the habits we've developed over time. *Nature cannot be changed, but it doesn't determine who we ultimately will be.* You can be easygoing and mellow or volatile and passionate as a *tzaddik* or as a *rasha*.[38] While the habits we must work on to change or improve may be determined by our inborn traits, what we become is not dictated by our nature, nor even by the habits we've developed over time.

As we said earlier, every person must ask himself: *Who am I?* If I measure my successes or failures on the basis of others, that's not me. If I measure my successes or failures on the basis of what I do, that's also not me; much of what I do (or don't do) is actually a result of my environment and education. None of that is really *me*. As I often tell my students, "You run a race against no one in life!"

So what — or who — is the real "me"?

When examining our lives to see if we are achieving our potential, we must be especially careful not to judge ourselves based on someone else's accomplishments. After all, the Midrash tells us, "Can a person see his comrade in the World to Come?"[39]

So who is the real "you"?

1. *The importance of tests: you are what you choose.* The *Gesher HaChaim* says[40] that the only true "I" is what I choose. *My choices define who I am.* My choices are unique to me, reflecting what is expected of me and what I can and cannot do.

When I do only what I've been brought up to do, I haven't found the real me; I've found my parents.[41] It's only when I'm confronted by a test, something that doesn't come easily be-

---

38. See *Divrei Yehoshua*, Ch. 4, *ma'amar* 2.
39. *Shemos Rabbah* 52:3.
40. *Gesher HaChaim* 3:4:2.
41. Rav Eliyahu Eliezer Dessler, *Michtav MeEliyahu*, vol. 1, pp. 115–16.

cause of my genetic background, my upbringing, and the habits that I have developed, and must choose how to respond that I can really find myself.

2. *The importance of effort: you are what you try.* The measure of a person is his willingness to work. My portion of anything I accomplish is really only the effort I invested in trying to achieve my goal. Rav Dessler teaches us that the place that a person earns in the Next World is a direct reflection of how hard he worked.[42]

3. *Your unique task: you are what you're here for.* Rav Tzadok HaKohen tells us[43] that even if we are successful at something, this doesn't necessarily mean that we're doing the right thing. We are all here for a specific reason; in fact, each moment has its specific purpose. The Sfas Emes explains[44] that the *mishnah* "*Im ein ani li mi li*— If I am not for myself, who will be for me?"[45] implies that my life's work can be done by no one but me.

How to discern our life's mission is a huge subject, but we need to know that it is unique to each one of us. If we have our priorities straight, if we have achieved a strong level of *yiras Hashem*, which opens us up to the desire to know what Hashem wants from us, then Hashem will help us achieve our potential.

---

42. Ibid., vol. 3, p. 21.

43. *Tzidkas HaTzaddik* 62.

44. *Bechukosai* 5632, s.v. "*adoni avi zekeini.*"

45. *Avos* 1:14.

Turning Ideas into Action

▶ *Take responsibility.*

Several times a year, determine which actions are results of your upbringing or environment. This is not to cast blame, but simply to recognize where they come from, and taking responsibility to change them if they are negative and giving credit when they are positive.

▶ *Savor the victories.*

I was told by the *mashgiach* Rav Shlomo Wolbe, *z"l*,[46] that nowadays *cheshbon hanefesh* — the spiritual accounting that every Jew who wants a proactive, spiritually successful life must make — means taking note of what we have done right that day. It would therefore be a beautiful exercise to make a list of these accomplishments, especially noting those that were difficult to achieve. Savor them, thanking Hashem for helping you achieve these not insignificant victories.

▶ *Acquire a positive habit.*

Once a month, take on a small, positive habit, such as wishing someone good morning or calling a loved one to let them know that they are on your mind, on your "radar." Each month, take time to notice if these habits have become more a part of you and have become easier.

---

46. Rav Wolbe specifically requested that he be referred to as *z"l*, "of blessed memory," and not *zt"l*, "the memory of the righteous is for a blessing."

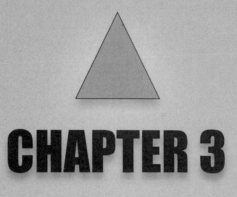

CHAPTER 3

The Parenting Mind-Set

Anger or Solutions: Bringing Down the Emotional Temperature

*E*very human being has what I call an "emotional temperature," and when it gets too high, problems develop! Any leader, and any parent, must be in control of his or her emotions. Let's learn how to prevent the next blowup.

Take charge

The Gerrer Rebbe, Rabbi Yehudah Leib Alter, *zt"l*, was once traveling abroad by train. His chassidim stayed with him until the border. When they took leave of him, they asked him to share a Torah thought with them. He said, "Do you know what gives the train's engine the ability to pull [i.e., lead] the rest of the cars along with it? It's because it can hold its steam [an analogy to anger] inside of him."[1]

The intellect must rule. Properly regulated emotional temperature is energy that the intellect can harness, and it is never set into action without the intellect's approval. Even when emotion is used — and indeed sometimes it must be used — it should be clear that the emotion stems from a deep intellectual conviction. No matter what, the person is in control.

What are some attitudes that we can develop to keep our "emotional temperature" under control?

Some failure is inevitable

Parents, for example, need to be conscious that there will be times when they will fail. Sometimes the problem doesn't lend itself to a simple, immediate solution, or they tried an approach that was wrong either for practical, technical reasons or for more fundamental reasons.

We are told that children are like the arrows of a marksman.[2] Just as a marksman doesn't score a "bull's-eye" every time he shoots, so it is with children: *there will be mistakes*. This is vital for us to know, since our ability to bounce back is enhanced by our knowledge that the failures are natural.

Basically, we are good!

One attitude that we often have is that we can't separate how well we do from how good we are. It is one of the basic

---

1. Taken from Rav Avraham Tobolsky, *V'Haser Ka'ascha MiLibcha* (Bnei Brak, 1978). I believe that the Hebrew word for "lead," as in "*yancheini* — He will lead me" (*Tehillim* 23:3) and "*v'lo nacham* — and He did not lead them" (*Shemos* 13:17), are both derivatives of *menuchah*, the word for peace and tranquillity. A leader needs to be calm and not let his emotions govern him.
2. See *Tehillim* 127:4.

tenets of Judaism that *the soul is inherently pure and our goodness is immutable.*

When a person realizes that his basic goodness — and the basic goodness of his child — is never at stake, he can calm down.

Can we live with it, at least temporarily?

Sometimes people feel an intense pressure to eliminate a problem — immediately. *There are few problems that must be solved both totally and immediately.* When a person realizes this, not only will his emotional temperature drop, but he can begin the path of true problem solving. Eventually, with Hashem's help, the situation will be resolved.

Reframe!

If something is disturbing you, try looking at it in a different way. Perhaps you are a punctual person and your wife "lives on the edge" when it comes to being on time. Next time you want to get to the *chuppah* and she hasn't even started getting dressed, think: perhaps your wife's more laid-back attitude to life, which often causes her to be late, is also responsible for the congenial atmosphere in your home that you so appreciate, an atmosphere that keeps your children happy and in the home, not on the streets or in questionable places.

Take care of yourself

Proper diet and sleep are integral to a calm, optimistic demeanor. The Rosh Yeshivah, *zt"l*, would compassionately tell people who come to him for advice, but were deeply overwhelmed and bitter over their troubles, "*Gei shloff zich oys* — Go get some sleep." He knew that tired people are unable to deal with their problems properly.

Is this really the problem?

Sometimes the problem really stems from a different, more emotion-filled source. For example, there can be a strong disagreement between spouses as to how to solve a specific child-rearing problem. The emotion doesn't come from the problem with the child, but from the "battle" with the spouse, with all the baggage that may come with it.

Also, sometimes, when there is a confrontation between a parent and child, the problem becomes determining who is "stronger" and who will "win" the battle. In such a situation, an unnecessary amount of emotion is invested and the emotional temperature goes up.

Where's your focus?

People tend to notice the negative. When a problem presents itself in a relationship, we often focus on the specific misbehavior without looking at the total person, sometimes overlooking his or her many redeeming traits. Emotion tends to be overwhelming, and there's little room for perspective. We need to see the person as a whole, and his or her behavior as a part of that whole, and then our emotional temperature will go down.

Be prepared for surprises

Emotional reactions are at the root of many of our mistakes, and *surprise is the high-octane gasoline that can fuel those emotions*. We must remember that life is like a golf course; the sand traps, high grass, and sudden winds are to be expected and hence should not throw us off from doing our best to achieve our goals. We should look at the totality of the life that Hashem has bestowed on us and consider these joys when preparing to solve problems with equanimity.

My paradigm of anger is frustration at the gap between the way I think things should be and the way they are. So don't be too sold on the "picture" of how things should be and your frustration, and anger, will be easier to manage.

Plan a reaction

Just as a fire drill prepares us for the real thing, when we have a planned reaction to a situation, we are calmer before entering it — and calmer in implementing it. Tell yourself what to expect, how you want to respond to the situation, and keep calm!

We are responsible, as adults, for harnessing our emotions and for keeping our emotional temperature under control. When we do, we will have the presence of mind to become the parents our children truly need and create a home environment our children want to live in and, eventually, emulate.

Mori V'Rabi, zt"l, used to say that you can get angry or you can accomplish something (such as solving the problem at hand) — but you can't do both.

Turning Ideas into Action ▶

▶ *Minimize the surprise.*

Once a day, before entering a new situation, try to clarify to yourself the purpose of the situation — i.e., what are you doing there in the first place. Then visualize what you can expect to encounter in that situation. This will help you avoid unnecessary surprises that can lead to anger.[3]

▶ *Internalize the message of Shabbos.*

On Shabbos we are meant to internalize that it is Hashem's world and we can trust Him totally. We should feel as if all our mundane work is done, and we can rely on Him for everything. This can be an important tool in enabling us to keep our emotions under control. At the third meal of Shabbos, try to retain the feelings of trust in Hashem that are part and parcel of Shabbos. Prepare to take these feelings with you into your week.[4]

▶ *Relax — take a nap.*

Make sure, before your children (or your spouse!) come home, to have something light and nutritious

---

3. This general advice appears in *Shem MiShmuel, Devarim*, p. 167.

4. This advice appears in *Shem MiShmuel, Bereishis*, p. 88.

to eat and to relax or take a short nap. This nap can last even a few moments. Even if you don't actually fall asleep, Professor Eli Davis of Hadassah Hospital told me that relaxed moments in a quiet, darkened environment can be worth up to 80 percent of proper sleep.

▶ *Contemplate your inner goodness.*

In the morning, before saying the words *"neshamah shenasata bi tehorah hi* — the soul You have placed in me is pure,"* stop and focus on the truth of these words. Try to internalize them before you begin your day.

The Jewish Family: Preserving and Enhancing It in a Turbulent World

*C*hild-rearing is always a challenge and can sometimes be painful. Here's what we need to know to turn the pain of child-rearing into a happy, if sometimes difficult, experience.

The importance of adapting

Before I begin, I would like to translate the title of this chapter and explain the rationale behind it. These definitions may sound abstract, but they are necessary in order that what follows — the practical side — will be anchored in what our Torah teaches us.

"The Jewish Family" — Rav Shlomo Wolbe, *z"l*, defines *family* as the bearer of the Divine Presence among the Jewish people.[5]

"Preserving" — retaining what was in the past.

"Enhancing It in a Turbulent World" — adapting the family to handle the unique challenges of the present.

It is the hallmark of this world that there will be change. The family needs flexibility to deal with the inevitable changes the future will bring. *This ability to adapt the old truths to new circumstances will be the test upon which the family will stand or fall.* I specifically use the word *enhancing* — which means "to raise to a higher degree" — since each generation's ability to withstand tests that the earlier generation didn't have to deal with brings an additional, new form of praise to Hashem, as it says, "Generation to generation will *improve* on Your praise."[6]

Let's take a look at the deeper meaning of these ideas.

"Family" — the bearer of the Divine Presence

A family is much more than a collection of people who are genetically related. As we have just said, Rav Wolbe states that the family is — or, rather, the family can and should be — the bearer of the *Shechinah*.

Two factors cause Hashem to rest His *Shechinah*, His Divine Presence, upon us and upon our homes:

1. *Happiness.* We are taught that the Divine Presence rests only in a place where there is joy.[7] This, Rav Wolbe says, is the source for the mitzvah of making a bride and groom happy. By doing so, we are bringing the *Shechinah* down to the new home, creating a new resting place for the *Shechinah*.[8] A home

---

5. *Alei Shur*, vol. 1, p. 255.

6. *Tehillim* 145:4.

7. *Shabbos* 30b; see *Maharal, Nesivos Olam, Nesiv HaTorah*, Ch. 18.

8. *Alei Shur*, vol. 1, p. 256.

that is imbued with *simchah,* joy, is a home where the *Shechi-nah* can come to rest.

2. *Household harmony — peace.* When a husband and wife have peace between them, the *Shechinah* dwells with them.[9]

If peace enables us to bring Hashem's Presence into our homes, it's important for us to understand just what *peace* means. Peace is not achieved by one person "surrendering" to the other and nullifying himself. Rav Wolbe defines *peace* as the ability to bridge differences.[10] *The idea of peace is to allow for the coexistence and balance of seeming opposites.*

This was the function of the twelve tribes coming together three times a year in Jerusalem. Each tribe was different, and in coming together they could achieve the balance that created a Yerushalayim — a "City of Peace."[11]

Even in the physical realm, we find this idea of balancing differences. Rav Eliyahu Eliezer Dessler, *zt"l,* defines health, both physical and spiritual, as the proper blending and balancing of various attributes. If one physical characteristic becomes too powerful at the expense of another one, the result will be illness. Too much of one enzyme or hormone will cause sickness. A limb or organ that is disproportionate to the rest of the body can lead to dysfunction.[12]

The word *ish* (איש), which means "an important and successful man," stands for אמצע ימין שמאל, "middle, right, left."

---

9. This lesson is apparent in the very words for "man" and "woman." The word for "woman" is *ishah* (אשה) and for "man" it is *ish* (איש). The *hei* of *ishah* and the *yud* of *ish* form Hashem's Name. When the Name is missing, the two words spell *eish* (אש), "fire." When there is fire and strife between a husband and wife, they chase away the Divine Presence. But when there is harmony between them, each one contributes to keeping the Divine Presence in the home.

10. *Alei Shur,* vol. 1, p. 257.

11. Heard from Rav Avigdor Miller, *zt"l.*

12. *Michtav MeEliyahu,* vol. 4, p. 251. See also *Sefer HaYashar,* beginning of Gate 7, for a lengthy discussion about the relationship between balance and physical health.

A true "*ish*" is someone who can balance extremes and bring them into the middle.[13]

How does this manifest in the home?

It is a given, in a home where there are several children, that each child will receive a different form of parental attention. This is especially true in a home where there is an ill or special-needs child. In such cases, when the physical, emotional, and financial needs of one child exceeds that of his siblings, parents need to balance this reality by making an effort to develop a special relationship with their other children.

They can do this by setting aside quality time alone with each child, when the child feels heard and understood without feeling that the parent is in a hurry to do something else instead. The parent should also express the desire to have more time and resources for each child and be ready to address any issues the child may have.

Also, when parents show that the efforts they expend for a sick or special-needs child is not a burden to be shirked, but is an expression of Hashem's will, they imbue *emunah* and *bitachon* in their other children. In this way, they help them accept the situation as a reality and not resent it. They can even include their children — without forcing them — in the attention and care they pay to the special-needs sibling.

Parents who are able to balance their need to attend to the more immediate and urgent needs of an ill child with the foresight of how this can enrich their other children's lives create a home of giving, joy, and peace.

Children will flourish in a home that is open to the Shechinah: a home characterized by happiness and by the balance of true harmony.

The next word in our title is *preserving*. When we apply it to family, it means retaining the characteristics of the traditional strong Jewish home, as it existed in previous times.

---

13. *Be'er Moshe, Bamidbar*, p. 658.

What are we preserving?

In earlier times, there was greater discipline in the home. Today we find that many parents and teachers are afraid to discipline children for fear that they will "go off the *derech*," that they will leave the traditional Torah path of their fathers. Is it true that the home has changed in its essence, that it is no longer a place of discipline? Is discipline too "dangerous" today?

The answer to those questions is a resounding no! *Discipline and limits must be a part of our child-rearing, just as they were in the past.*

We have defined peace as balance, the ability to combine seeming opposites. We said that one way this is manifest is when the parents make sure to fulfill the needs of each child. Another way this is manifest is by balancing discipline with love. In a peaceful home, the children benefit from two opposite approaches, which together enable them to grow fully and well: a left hand that pushes while a right hand pulls closer.[14] This is what we must work to preserve.

So how do we do it?

Preserving the balance

Love and discipline can coexist when there are three traits underpinning the relationship between child and parent:
1. respect and
2. trust,
which lead to
3. obedience.

A child needs to know that his parents know more than he does — not about the latest technology, but about the truths of life. He must *respect* his parents' judgment and opinion. How do we inculcate respect?

---

14. See *Sanhedrin* 107b.

It cannot be overstated that we must conduct ourselves in a manner deserving of respect. We can't lose ourselves in anger; we must speak respectfully to our spouse. This is a given, and I will not elaborate on it.

With regard to our relationship with our children, in earlier days the "left hand" pushed children "away"; that is, there was a clear distance between a parent and child. The child was not an equal. He could not sit in a parent's place, and he could not contradict a parent. There was dignity and distance.

Obviously, this distance must be in accord with the times we live in (few parents would ask their children to kiss their hands today, as they did in olden times), but we must remember that we are not our children's friends, we are their parents — and we must realize that this *sense of dignity is for our child's benefit*. A child wants to respect a parent, because his own self-respect is intertwined with how he feels about his parents.

> In the United States, at the beginning of the last century, many children were lost to *Yiddishkeit* because they lacked respect for their parents. How could children look up to their parents when the parents didn't even look up to themselves? They were, in their own words, *"greener"* — greenhorns who hardly spoke English and didn't understand America. Many felt almost in awe of their children, who were so much more comfortable in their new reality.

Nowadays, even though most parents are well educated and at home in society, another obstacle to respect has presented itself: technology. In addition to the many dangers of the Internet, which is not the subject here, there is another more subtle problem: many young people are much more at home with the world of high-tech than adults, and often they look with disdain or pity on their "ignorant" parents, who must turn to them to figure out how to download an MP3.

Preserving our dignity may not be easy today, but it is essential.

Just as important, the child must truly believe that his parents bear his welfare in mind; he must deeply *trust* them.

> Going back to our example from early 20th-century America, many of the European immigrants operated under the motto "My son the doctor." They were interested in having *nachas* from their children, often without considering what would be best for the child. The outcome of this became all too clear — the children often rejected their parents' heritage — their *Yiddishkeit* — and often distanced themselves from the parent as well. To use Mori V'Rabi's words, "My son the doctor caused the generation gap."

> Today, again, we see this phenomenon in a somewhat different form. Unfortunately, I sometimes meet parents who have to be reminded that their children are not "*nachas* machines." Even with something as vital as success in school, the child must know that the parent isn't looking for the honor that comes with being the mother or father of a top student; rather, the parent wants the child to succeed, or to do as well as he is able, for his sake alone.

When respect and trust are firmly in place, there will be *obedience*, and we will have preserved the best of our Jewish past.

Now, for the third part of our title:

"Enhancing the family in a turbulent world"

The world has always been turbulent but the institution of family hasn't, and the degree and rapidity of change wasn't as breathless as it is today.

Here are some things that parents need to do to navigate the perilous waters of contemporary child-rearing:

Parents need da'as Torah. Now, more than ever, parents must have someone to consult who has some level of *da'as Torah,* an approach and direction grounded in Torah scholarship and wisdom. It is best if the person they consult knows the family well and understands the family dynamic and the child under discussion. Don't wait until a crisis erupts; "make for yourself a *rav,*"[15] create a relationship with someone whose *da'as Torah* you can trust while things are relatively tranquil.

Parents need other parents. When your children are behaving in ways that leave you puzzled, confused, or angry, ask parents of other children who are in similar situations what they've done that worked (or didn't work!). This isn't *da'as Torah,* but rather utilizing other people as a sounding board and learning from their experiences. Perhaps you've missed something or haven't tried something that worked for someone else in the same situation. (Remember, however, that what worked in one family may not necessarily work in a different one.)

Parents need to pray. And they need to believe in the power of those *tefillos* to change what seems to be an unchangeable situation.

Parents need to believe. They need to believe in the essential goodness of themselves and their child.

> I knew a wonderful woman who lived through the horror of Auschwitz. Once, when we spoke, she recalled a turning point in her life. She had begun to frequent the Shabbos get-togethers of the local non-religious Zionist youth in her Hungarian town. People in the town visited her grandfather, the *rav* of the community, to inform him of what his granddaughter was doing. She overheard his reply: "My Yehudis would never do such a thing. It cannot be." Upon hearing those words she

---

15. *Avos* 1:6.

resolved never to return to those gatherings. She could never disappoint her grandfather, who truly believed in her. She survived the war and raised two amazing children, both dedicated to the welfare of the Jewish people.

We must remember that what the home is going through today is an expression of Hashem's will. We didn't set up the world this way, and we are not responsible for how the world looks. What is in our control is to do our best in the circumstances in which Hashem has placed us.

Let us give our children and ourselves these anchors: discipline, respect, trust, and belief in ourselves and in them.

Turning Ideas into Action

▶ *Create an atmosphere of respect in your home.*

Respect — showing that "you matter to me" — is a bulwark of a happy, secure atmosphere for a child. For the husband: Before returning home each evening, make a mental note to greet your wife warmly and to sincerely thank her for dinner or anything else she did for you that day. When she speaks to you, give her your full attention and respond respectfully to whatever matter she raises. For the wife: When your husband enters the home, greet him warmly and happily. When he has settled down, ask him sincerely how his day went.

▶ Also show respect for the children: When children make requests, hear them out and take the time to consider their requests, repeating back to them what they are feeling and requesting. They will accept a No far more graciously because their request was given sincere genuine consideration. Just try not to say No too often. Sometimes, fulfilling part of a request is in order. Too-frequent No's will result in children doing without asking!

▶ *Feel the joy of being dependent on Hashem.*

It is a great happiness to know that you are in His powerful, loving hands. Take a few moments each day to sincerely ask Hashem for His blessing in all of your undertakings for your children. This can be close to the time that the children are due home. Make up your mind that any success you have with your children will not cause you to feel arrogant, and you will never be judgmental of others who are having less success with their children.

▶ **Seek da'as Torah.**

If there seems to be a negative pattern developing with a child, make sure that you have a connection to a *rav* who knows your family and can give you guidance. Older, more experienced parents can also be helpful, provided that they realize that what worked for them will not necessarily work for you.

Home and Family:
An Invincible Pair

O *nce upon a time we lived in the shtetl, a place that protected us from the spiritual dangers of the outside world. Those days are over, and today we and our children contend daily with alarming and frightening assaults on our Torah faith and values. Changing times require fresh strategies and redoubled efforts to harness the power of our traditional strengths. One of the greatest of these strengths is the Jewish home, which Rav Shlomo Wolbe, z"l, called "the bearer of the Divine Presence" among the Jewish people.[16] Today our defense systems are the double-barreled power of the Jewish home and the strength of our family ties.*

Make the most of your assets

There is an important principle of child-raising that we can learn from marketing and advertising professionals:

---

16. *Alei Shur*, vol. 1, p. 55. See also Mind-Set 11 above.

A delegation from the Israeli government was touring Ohr Somayach, a well-known yeshivah for young men looking to reclaim their Jewish heritage. When they heard that there was a public-relations expert among the students, they asked to meet him. One of the government officials asked him how he would recommend they "sell" Israel. He answered, "You will never find a product whose advertising theme is 'Our product is as good as our competitor's.' Marketers seek to emphasize that which is unique to their product. Israel should not market itself on the basis of its secular entertainment. You could find bigger and better distractions in many other places. Israel should market that which makes it so special — spirituality."

This principle, that we must compete in the areas where we are strongest, is one of the most fundamental strategies I know for protecting our children from the negative influences that surround them. Like a country that wants to increase its exports, we must find the products that we excel in that are missing in the marketplace. *To compete with "the street," we must find the things that our children need most*, things that the street is far less equipped to give them.

So what is it that our children need most? What can they get from us that they can't get from the secular world out there? What product do we have to offer them?

The home and the family: An invincible pair

Parents and siblings must know that they have no competition out there. What they can give can't be duplicated. *When you give your child or your brother and sister time, understanding, and acceptance, the connection will never be broken permanently.* Like all relationships, especially close ones, there can be stormy moments, but after all is said and done, the security of a happy, loving home is unique. There may be times when a child will, out of frustration and anger, do infuriating things, but the bond will never be severed.

> A man I knew who had recently divorced had custody of his 11-year-old son. He placed him in a Torah school. The mother had custody for one weekend a month and would take the child with her to Las Vegas. How could the father compete with Las Vegas and the terribly immoral lessons his son might learn there?
>
> The answer was clear. He needed to compete where he was strong. It was impossible to give the child more "fun" than he would find in Las Vegas. But he could give the child a warm, loving, and interested father. In this, Las Vegas could never begin to rival what the father had at his disposal.
>
> Several years have passed since this question arose. The father triumphed, and his son, recognizing where his home truly was, has espoused his father's values. Today the boy is a true *ben Torah*. The father beat Las Vegas.

A great educator once shared with me a remark that his son had made to him. The boy, a teenager, was not interested in the intensive Torah study that is the hallmark of many children in today's Torah-true homes. "But don't worry, Abba," he told his father, "even though Torah study doesn't pull me, I'm not going to go off and leave a Torah-observant lifestyle. I know that you love me."

Rav Yechiel Yakobson, one of Israel's revered educators, once met with a group of "off-the-track" teenagers. He asked them how he could prevent what happened in their families happening in his own. They answered, "The Rav doesn't have to worry. His children know that he loves them."

At a wedding in Milwaukee, I sat at the same table as Rav Michel Twerski, *shlita*, who grew up in Milwaukee 80 years ago and attended public school, since there were no yeshivos there at the time. During the course of our conversation, I asked him how he and his brothers turned out to be such wonderful disseminators of Torah and, even more, such paragons of Torah principles and Torah living. When I asked the question, his entire demeanor changed. Slowly and clearly he said something that has never left me. "We knew two things about our father: that he loved us very much and that he believed in us."

How we truly feel about our children, the respect we have for them and their feelings and ideas, coupled with a great and intense love, is the best guarantee we have that they will follow our closest held beliefs.

This is not to say that families where children have left traditional Judaism do not or did not love their children. But, sometimes, despite the parents' best efforts, the message that they love their children does not come through clearly.

That said, we must remember that we can never judge a family by how the children "turned out." The Satmar Rav, *zt"l*, commented that the saying "The apple never falls far from the tree" is not true when there are hurricane winds outside. Indeed, there is a hurricane out there, with a world gone crazy, seeking pleasure with insane abandon.

Getting the message through

We said that sometimes the message that parents love their children does not come through clearly. Why not?

One reason is that *sometimes children perceive that the love of their parents is conditional.* They think that their parents' love is predicated on their doing or being something. This love is often rejected, and hatred eventually takes its place. This can happen if the parents' love, acceptance, and respect are contingent on how much their child has accomplished, whether professionally or academically, on how helpful the child is to them, or how religious the child is.

Mori V'Rabi, *zt"l*, said that the "generation gap" of decades ago stemmed from "My son the doctor." The parents made their measure of their child's success and their "*nachas*" and pride in him contingent on his becoming a doctor or lawyer. The child sensed that his parents were not putting his interests first, and thus the generation gap developed.

Parents are treading on thin ice when they tie their love, respect, and acceptance too tightly to any particular thing, even success in Torah observance and Torah study — as vital and irreplaceable as that is for a successful life in both this world and the next.

Here is an excerpt from a letter sent to the above-mentioned Rav Yakobson from a child who had run away from home. The letter speaks for itself and is worthy of our close attention:

> I don't care about him [my father] because he doesn't truly care about me. Only when I brought him recognition or good grades, or when I would help him a lot — only then would he smile at me, and once, perhaps twice, he even hugged me and kissed me... He would become enraged and hit me when I went to my aunt, since they are not so religious. But I went, because my aunt always smiled at me. I would just open the door and she would already smile at me and was glad that I had come and would hug me as if I were her own son, even when I hadn't done something good to deserve it.

The youngster who wrote this letter was quite certain his father did not love him. It is likely that he was totally wrong; his father almost certainly did (and hopefully still does) love his child. Parents naturally love their children. But that love, at least in the boy's eyes, was contingent on achievement, and that just wasn't enough.

This does not mean that there is never a situation when one should chastise, and perhaps even distance, a child, but this must be done only with the complete agreement of a capable *rav* who understands the full implications of taking this action.

Generally, a lack of mitzvah observance is not in and of itself grounds for sending a child away from home. If he or she is becoming a bad influence on the younger children, advice from a *gadol b'Torah* needs to be sought, with a clear presentation of all the valid aspects of the situation.

> As an example of just how serious a child's behavior must be to distance him from home, I was told about a 7-year-old child who, when angry, would pull a knife on his 4-year-old sister and say he was going to kill her. Clearly, the child needed professional help, but the behavior had to be stopped immediately. I advised the parents to pack a suitcase, show it to him, and firmly but lovingly tell the child he had a choice: either stop traumatizing his sister, or they would have to find him another place to live. It was his choice. Everyone wanted him home. But if he chose to continue to threaten his sister, he would have to leave, at least temporarily, while he thought things over.

Obviously, this case is an extreme one, and thankfully it occurred only once in the more than 35 years that I have been involved in *chinuch*. But its severity serves to highlight several important principles. Two simultaneous messages needed to be sent to the child:

1. We love you and want you home, and would never want you to leave our family. However,

2. there are redlines in life. You have the ability to restrain yourself from crossing those redlines, and when you do, it is

your choice. When you cross them, you are bringing the previously agreed-upon consequences on yourself.

It cannot be overemphasized that this is not a battle between the parent and child. It is the parent demanding that the child be responsible for behavior that crosses redlines, such as compromising the safety of his siblings.[17] And there shouldn't be too many redlines: a home is not a minefield.

Speaking the same language

Another reason that the parents' love for their children doesn't come through clearly is that *sometimes children and parents "speak different languages."* Sometimes a parent thinks he is conveying love when a child is "hearing" something entirely different.

In the letter mentioned above, the child emphasized how much being hugged meant to him. Even though his father surely loved him, the child needed the hug, which the father rarely gave, to feel it. Since their "languages" were different, the child thought his father didn't care about him.

For various reasons, some adults, particularly men, don't express love by touch. They rarely kiss or hug. This is fine; there are other ways we can express affection. The problem arises when they live with someone (either a spouse or a child)

---

17. If the child can't stick to those redlines on his own, then prevention is necessary, as we prevent a 2-year-old from harming an infant sibling. This, however, is a technical necessity and not *chinuch*, which happens when the child internalizes life truths and modes of behavior and then disciplines himself to adhere to them. It's the parents' primary responsibility to protect the infant, *not* to "educate" the 2-year-old. Remaining alert, looking for patterns of when the toddler will seek to hurt his sibling, seeking to distract the child, and *removing the infant* from the toddler's presence are the basic strategies that are called for here. But don't get into a battle with the 2-year-old, such as sending him to his room to "teach him how to treat his sister," because then you are giving the child the option to oppose you and you may be in for a long, strenuous confrontation, which the child may actually win. See Mind-Set 15 for more on confrontations with children.

who needs to be hugged and kissed at some level of frequency. Words of affection or actions that demonstrate affection are not always "heard." As far as the child is concerned, there is a deafening silence, a relationship that is devoid of love. Again, it may be totally untrue, the parent may feel deep love, but it is not coming across.

A situation that I was involved in showed me how deep these misunderstandings can go. A child felt his mother didn't love him. This woman loved her child so intensely that she wrote him little loving notes and put them in his lunch box. And yet this gesture of love was totally lost on the child, who needed more than anything else to be hugged.

Transforming your communications

What can be done when the child needs touch, when he needs hugging and kissing, and the parent simply doesn't speak that language?

In the world of electricity, when you have an appliance that runs on 110 volts and you are plugging it into a wall outlet that sends 220 volts, you need a transformer, or else the appliance will be destroyed in seconds by a level of current it can't handle. In effect, the transformer acts as a "translator," changing the "language" that the electricity source "speaks" to one that the appliance can "hear."

The same holds true in the world of relationships. When two people speak two different emotional languages, they need to learn, recognize, and respect the language of the other. When they recognize each other's language and realize that love is being expressed, they can then use their "transformer" and understand that they are loved.

Children, though, are often not emotionally mature enough to do this "translating." If that's the case, the parent needs to be more creative and search for ways to show love, whether it's by reading stories to the child or taking the child out of school occasionally to buy him or her an ice cream.

Teaching children to "freeze" the good times

I remember the story of an older child who was frustrated because his father praised him so rarely. The father was a reserved man, and the praise, when it finally came, was much more muted and low-key than the child would have liked.

The child was told to do two things to help him deal with the situation:

1. *"Translate" your father's words.* When the father would say, in a low voice, "That was fine," the boy should translate that into a shout that said, "That was GREAAAT!" This was not a falsification at all, just an adjustment from the father's 110 current to the child's 220.

2. *"Freeze" the moment.* When there was a warm interchange between the father and the son, the son should remember it in great detail. What did the environment look like? Was it light or dark, warm or cold, day or night? The memory could then be pulled out in its entirety, and the situation relived, complete with the good feelings.[18]

Teaching our children these two techniques can go a long way into helping our communication, even when we need "translation" and "transformers."[19]

It may even be possible for the parent to learn to hug. Not a cold, forced one, but a real one, the kind the child so desperately wants. How?

---

18. I tell newlyweds to do the same: to "freeze" the appreciation and love that they feel for their spouse — to recall the situation in its entirety and then to pull out those memories during the tougher times.

19. The above suggestions, however, may be very difficult for a young child, or even a preteen, to do. If that's the case, then the onus of creating a more positive relationship rests solely on the parent.

Shared reality

When you care about someone, that person's feelings can be transmitted to you, and you can share his emotional reality.

When one of my male students marries, I often give the following advice:

If your wife wants to go with you to buy drapes, and you aren't a bit interested in which kind of drapes she buys, you have three choices of action:

1. *Don't go.* That would be a mistake.

2. *Go and pretend you are interested.* That would be an even bigger mistake. Wives have powerful "antennas" and can be hurt when the interest is forced and artificial.

3. *Go and be interested.* How can you be interested in something that you aren't interested in? By feeling, "If it's important to you, it's important to me."

Whether it's with your spouse or your children, when you truly feel that what's important to them is important to you, you will soon find yourself communicating your love — and the message will get through.

Winning — against all odds

In a hospital ward people must be more careful with their diet and sleep patterns than they were when they were well; they need to maintain a higher level of resistance to infection than they normally would outside the hospital. So, too, with our children in today's world. *Parents need to invest more time and love than was perhaps necessary in past generations.* The "germs" of the street require that we fortify our children even more than was previously thought necessary.

Our homes need to be places of happiness, encouragement, and nurturing. Then there is much cause for optimism that children will choose the home over the street.

Turning Ideas into Action ▶

▶ *Find common ground.*

Even parents who have a different nature than their children can find common ground in activities that interest both of them. Think of activities you enjoy that you might have in common with your children, and ask your children to think of some as well. For example:

1. Plan a trip together to a place of mutual interest. It's the planning itself that fosters bonding, provided that it doesn't cause unpleasant disagreements.

2. Organize a "learning project." You should plan it together with your child, and it should have the following facets:

   a. It should have small bite-size measures of accomplishment, such as a chapter of *Nach*, a *perek* of a shortish tractate of Mishnah, or some halachos that have a daily relevance, such as *berachos* ("How many *berachos* do you make over chocolate-covered peanuts?"). The child will get a sense of accomplishment and enjoy the short bits of time with his parent.

   b. Some mini-celebration should follow each small milestone of achievement.

   c. After completing the project, go together to a *rav* whom the child respects to get a test and recognition from the *rav* for the learning he did.

d. A mother can do the same thing with her child, if Torah study will be a bonding experience for them both! Just because she doesn't learn Mishnah and Gemara does not mean there isn't plenty to learn with her child, and certainly a daughter: relevant sections of the *Kitzur Shulchan Aruch*, *sifrei mussar*, *Chumash*, and *Navi* are among some areas of Torah that they can learn together. Afterward, it may be more appropriate to go to a woman whom the family respects rather than to a *rav*, unless the father accompanies them.

▶ *Maximize your business trips.*

Parents who travel on business can sometimes bring a child (one or, at most, two!) with them, depending, of course, on several things:

1. The age of the child and his temperament,

2. whether there are other people in that location, such as relatives, who can care for the child while the parent is attending to his affairs, and

3. the length of the trip. It shouldn't be too long or tiring, and the child should be able to keep pace with his class work while away, at least in some subjects.

Be sure to devote a day or half day at the beginning of the trip to have free time with your child. If you leave your time with the child for the end of the trip, something unexpected may come up and it may not happen. In this case, leave the best for first!

Above all, bear in mind that the time spent with your child when traveling is at least as important as the business that needs to be attended to. If you are more stressed than usual when you are on a business trip, then this is not a good idea for you. Remember, you are looking to bond with a child who may have a different temperament than yours, and special occasions can often provide that link. When you are together in a strange place, then it is more likely you will become closer. The situation presents opportunities to focus on the child that don't arise at home.

▶ *Alternatively, make a family visit.*

Consider taking your child along on an out-of-town visit to relatives whom you don't get to see often. Such a visit shouldn't take the child out of school for too long. You can take your child shopping in preparation for the trip and share the decision-making with him, provided the child is mature enough to give appropriate input.

Parenting: Three Expressions of Love

O ur community is plagued by the phenomenon of angry teens who repay the loving care they received with anger and a rejection of everything their parents hold dear. It seems that sometimes the message that we love them doesn't come across. What's the formula for letting our children see the depth of our love and commitment to them?

The active ingredient

The Torah accords great value to giving and contributing to the community, whether by teaching and disseminating Torah or attending to the needs of a community's poor, sick, or troubled. Yet there is another, darker side to this: one of the most common problems that busy, altruistic parents face is that their children sometimes feel a lack of parental attention.

Later in life, many of these children express the feeling that they were competing with the good deeds of their parents. This does not augur well for their wanting to continue in their parents' righteous footsteps, nor does it make for a healthy parent-child relationship.

One encounter with such a child stands out in my mind. A young man in his late teens told me that he could not bring himself to even open, much less study, any of his father's published works. He felt that these books had cost him his father.

At the same time, many great, altruistic families have succeeded in raising beautiful, dedicated, and loving children. Moreover, this success has been, to some degree, because of — not despite — their occupation with community affairs. These children have seen their parents' example and been inspired by it. Can we find, perhaps, the "active ingredient," the element that transformed resentment of a busy parent into the desire to emulate that parent?

Three life rules for communicating love

There is no question that *the feeling of being loved and respected by his parents is one of the decisive elements that will cause a child to espouse or, chalilah, reject his parents' value system.* If we could see how great men and women who were devoted to the needs of the community were able to communicate these feelings to their children, then we — even those of us not so burdened — can utilize these ideas to inspire our children to emulate us and value all that we hold dear.

Rav Reuven Feinstein, *shlita*, related to Rav Paysach Krohn, *shlita*, how he knew, as a young boy, that his overwhelmingly busy father, Rav Moshe Feinstein, *zt"l*, loved him dearly. Rav Krohn recorded Rav Reuven's impressions in one of his wonderful *Maggid* books.[20]

---

20. *In the Footsteps of the Maggid* (Mesorah Publications, 1992), p. 123.

Rav Reuven mentioned three things his father did that conveyed, without words, the message of love and respect that every child and, indeed, every human being needs. These three things, which remained engraved in Rav Reuven's memory, can serve as a paradigm for three basic rules in parenting in particular and in human relationships in general. I can't know whether Rav Moshe, *zt"l*, consciously had in mind these three rules, but for me, and hopefully for others, they will serve as an aid to internalize these three life lessons.

The first life rule: caring for physical needs — without being asked

Rav Reuven remembers how, on cold wintry New York City mornings, his father would enter young Reuven's room and place the clothes that Reuven would be wearing that day for school on the radiator. When Reuven awoke, he could enjoy the pleasure of putting on warm clothes on a winter's day. Reuven knew that his father was taking special care that he should be warm. Doing this in an original way showed Reuven that his father had taken the time to reflect on how he could make Reuven more comfortable, even though Rav Moshe was so busy with the needs of the Jewish people.[21]

This is in keeping with what Rav Moshe, *zt"l*, told his student, Rav Pinchos Weiner, *zt"l*. A teacher, said Rav Moshe, must show that he cares for his student's physical welfare, in order that the student will also believe that the teacher is truly concerned for his spiritual welfare.

---

21. Later I heard in Rav Reuven's name that his father did not want his child to develop a negative association between getting up to don cold clothing in the frigid air and going to learn Torah.

This concept brings to mind a beautiful story:

> Rav Moshe Schneider, *zt"l*, tells of a famous, brilliant professor who refused to convert to Christianity, despite the fact that he was not at all observant and conversion would greatly enhance his career prospects. When asked why he stubbornly refused to leave the Jewish people, he related the following:
>
> He came to Radin as a young boy, hoping to be accepted into the famous yeshivah of the Chafetz Chaim. It was right after Succos, and there were many candidates waiting to be tested. His first day in Radin went by without a test, and he was forced to stay in town overnight. Having no place to go, he decided to sleep on one of the benches in a local shul. It was cold. An elderly man entered the shul, and seeing the boy lying on a cold bench, he removed his coat, despite the cold, and covered him. The entire night the old man paced the cold shul and learned with a sweet tune, and his coat warmed the sleeping boy.
>
> The old man was the Chafetz Chaim.
>
> "Many times I was tempted to convert," said the professor, "but whenever I thought about that memorable night, I would say to myself, *From such a nation I cannot part ways.*"

The second life rule: If it's important to you, it's important to me

When Rav Reuven was young, the family stayed at a farm in the Catskill Mountains. There wasn't that much for a little boy to do. Once a day, however, the hotel owner would drive his truck to town to pick up supplies. The back of the truck was cushioned with hay, and the children would climb in for their daily ride. The roads were poorly paved, and the ride was blessedly bumpy.

Rav Reuven had a daily learning session with his father. If the truck was ready to leave during that learning period, Rav Moshe would stop and tell his son that they could continue later. He didn't want his son to miss the truck ride.

This, to me, is the paradigm of a second principle for communicating love to a child: "What is important to you — no matter how childish — is important to me." Rashi tells us[22] that the word *yada*, "know," connotes "to be beloved." You can't love someone you don't know.

The effort that Rav Moshe made to try to understand his child, to be aware of the things that were important to him, was a powerful nonverbal way to express love. There is a direct relationship between effort and love, and when a child knows that a busy parent puts thought into what is important to him, this is a clear message: I love you, and despite all my preoccupations, you are on my mind.[23]

The third life rule: Treat your children as well as you treat your guests

The third thing that Rav Reuven saw was that he almost never lost his place near his father at the Shabbos table, even though Rav Moshe often hosted important, world-famous

---

22. On *Bereishis* 18:19.

23. As an aside, we see that Rav Moshe was not afraid to end a learning session if he felt that his child would benefit from it in the long run. For the same reason, I generally advise fathers who are studying with their children to stop five minutes before the child wants to. That way, children have positive memories of the learning sessions, always remembering wanting to go on, never viewing them as a drag. If the child wants to learn for less than five minutes, this is a separate problem that needs to be addressed.

guests. This, I believe, is an example of a third important principle in parenting.

Children have a powerful sense of justice. If your behavior at home varies greatly when there are guests at home from when the family is alone, then your child will, at some point, cease to respect you.

We are generally respectful and accommodating to our guests. *Our children are our most important guests.* They, too, will be moving out when they become adults. While we need not (and perhaps must not) treat our children exactly the same way we treat other guests, we must remain as calm and good natured and patient with them as we are with others. If we are well known and held in good esteem in the community, but the child does not see this reflected in the home, then the stage is set, *chalilah*, for the child to reject not only the father, but the society that reveres him.

Rav Reuven felt that the love of his father was consistent. It made no difference whether someone outside the family was there or not. It was the same wonderful, caring, and nurturing relationship whether onlookers were present or not.

Our Sages have taught us that Torah is acquired by our creating *simanim*, memory aids, by which we can retain the lessons that we have learned. Perhaps these three pointers, given to us by one of our generation's greatest men, can help us remember some of the basic truths of child-rearing and, indeed, of all human relationships.

Turning Ideas into Action ▶

▶ *Take advantage of the Shabbos table.*

The Shabbos table is a prime opportunity for creating a warm, respectful relationship between parent and child. It is a magnificent opportunity for the child to speak and be heard, and it is a place where his thoughts are given respectful consideration. For example:

1. Use this opportunity to show interest in what is important to your child. Ask your child what song he would like to sing, or tell a story that is relevant to your child's age and interests. This attention sends a powerful, nonverbal message of respect to the child and can build up the child's sense of self-esteem.

2. Raise a question at the table and then take answers from the people at the meal. It should be a question that the child can relate to and one that he has a reasonable chance of giving a valid answer to. Questions can be on the parashah that the child has learned or an interesting halachic point that the child is familiar with, such as the laws of returning lost objects. Any answer that the child offers should be seriously considered, though sometimes his answer needs to be "clarified," meaning that the parent can add to the answer and transform it into an excellent thought.

3. Conversely, don't raise issues with adult guests that are too abstract for the child. This is akin to speaking a language the child doesn't understand. In addition to being disrespectful, it is a surefire way to create discipline problems at the table.

In short, the Shabbos table gives us the opportunity to show our children that what they think is important to us. We hear them out and consider what they say. Not only is this a way of creating a loving bond, it demonstrates to the child that listening to what someone says and showing him respect is not a sign of weakness, because even his parents do it. A child does not want to appear weak; if his parents listen to others and respect what they say, the child can do it, too.

▶ *Make learning sessions pleasant.*

In today's world, love of Torah is not an extra, a good thing for your child to have: it is absolutely vital. If the child will not love Torah (or mitzvos), then he or she is likely to love something else, and that something else can be deadly. So when learning Torah with a child, make sure that it's a positive experience. The parent should not be learning with a child only in order to improve his/her grades. Nowadays, it's not a parent's job to tutor his children when they are having difficulties in school. Most parents are too emotionally involved with their child's academic progress (or lack of it), and the potential conflict that could result is more damaging to him than the poor grade he might receive.[24] Instead, as suggested in Mind-Set 12, consider undertaking a "private" learning project — a project that

---

24. If the problem stems from a learning disability, the parent often isn't even equipped to help the child. This is particularly common when teaching a child how to read. If it's not going well, get a trained person to teach reading privately. Sometimes it's wise to take your child for a professional evaluation to determine what, if any, learning disability or handicap is present. With reading issues, eye-coordination problems need to be addressed so that learning to read will not become a laborious and unpleasant undertaking.

does not not revolve around something that the child is learning in school. Pick something that you are also interested in learning.

Don't worry about how much ground you cover. This has the advantage of enabling you to learn at your own pace — and the pace of your child. You can also use this opportunity to train your child to review properly. Make sure the experience is a joyful and successful one for your child. Often, the child forms a bond with that particular area of Torah, since we all love things we succeed at.

▶ *Display your love for Torah to your children.*

This, in turn, will instill a love for Torah in them. Children are dominated by emotion and are deeply affected by what they see.[25] It is therefore a good idea for fathers to spend a few moments studying Torah in front of their children, especially young children who can't yet learn themselves. Hold them on your lap or have them sit next to you. Stroke the child gently while learning with a pleasant tune. You can even begin with a day-old child!

---

25. Rabbi Paysach Krohn describes (*Along the Maggid's Journey* [Mesorah Publications, 1995], pp. 69–70) how an exceptionally diligent person passed away and didn't leave behind a single child who carried on his father's dedication to intense Torah learning. When questioned as to why, the children replied that whenever their father learned, he closed the door to his study and they weren't permitted to enter. Rabbi Krohn quoted the Belzer Rav, *zt"l*, as saying that this is what is meant by the verse "The hidden matters are for Hashem, our G-d, and the open ones are for us and our children forever" (*Devarim* 29:8). If you want something to be "for your children," if you want them to make it part of their souls, it has to be open and seen, not hidden behind closed doors. I would add to this that perhaps the children saw Torah study as their competitor for their father's attention, and they consistently "lost out" on their father because of his dedication to learning. This would, at the very least, have created in them an apathy for Torah learning.

Be a Great Communicator... to Your Kids

*A*mazing, isn't it, the number of times we tell kids things and they just don't seem to get it. Sometimes there is a feeling (a very frustrating one) that we are talking and no one is listening. They are our children, and therefore they must be brilliant, good natured, and wonderful — so why don't they listen? They seem to be able to listen and "get it" when their friends talk! Is there something wrong?

Yes, there is!

Words are not enough

I was once approached by a parent who was having problems with his 6-year-old. I asked what he had tried before seeing me. He said that he would lecture his child and tell him in no uncertain terms that what he was doing was wrong. I asked him if this had helped when he, the parent, had been a child, and he said that it hadn't. He also admitted that this approach wasn't working with his child either. Why did he continue to do this? I asked. He said he didn't know what else to do.

Of course we need to talk to our children. We use words all the time, speaking to even very young children, even infants. But we must remember that *talking is not the primary way that we communicate our most important messages to our children.* Because they are more emotional than adults, children react more readily to nonverbal messages.

As I said, this does not mean that we shouldn't speak to our children. Certainly words are ultimately a primary way of communication, but even verbal communication has strong nonverbal components.

Rav Shlomo Wolbe, *z"l,* in a remarkable exposition on speech, refers to proper speech as a harp.[26] Just as when someone plays a harp, a combination of many factors give the sound its proper resonance, so effective speech is made up of a combination of the words spoken, the emotion behind the words, and the character of the speaker. The emotions and the character of the speaker are powerful nonverbal components in maximizing the effectiveness of our speech.

If our words carry greater import when the nonverbal parts of speech are utilized in communication between adults, then certainly this is true when we speak to our children. It is important, therefore, to define the nonverbal parts of speech that can give impetus to our words. Let us mention the most important ones.

---

26. *Pelech HaShetikah V'Hahodayah* ("The Art of Silence and Praise"), Elul 5739 (1979).

Tone of voice

The Gemara tells us[27] that the members of our household accept authority when words are spoken softly. *A soft tone of voice suggests self-control, and people are more likely to follow someone who is in control of himself.* A person may shout hysterically that he is in control of himself, but the nonverbal message is far more powerful, and it is the one that will leave its mark.

Eye contact

Rav Yitzchok Hutner, *zt"l*, tells us that a person's emotional reality is apparent in his eyes, as the saying goes, "The eyes are the window to the soul."[28] *When we make eye contact, we are accessing the deepest recesses of the person.* It is for this reason that a look into someone's eyes is considered an emotional message, whether of love or hatred. Let us make soft, loving eye contact with our children when we speak to them. Not an unrelenting stare, but enough to transmit our nonverbal emotions to them.

Eye contact can also have powerful negative effects.

> A wonderful friend of mine, a well-known educator in Jerusalem, was walking down a street in Manhattan and made eye contact with a homeless man sitting on a stoop. The person leaped up and said, his voice full of hostility, "I could kill you now and everyone would understand." My friend apologized profusely, and, thank G-d, the man let him go on his way.

Eye contact is a powerful tool of communication. Let us use it wisely.

---

27. *Gittin* 6b; *Shabbos* 34a.

28. Rav Hutner cites this well-known aphorism in a letter published in *Iggros U'Kesovim* 136.

Touch

The Vilna Gaon teaches us[29] that touch is a primary means of transmitting emotion. When touch is coupled with earnest words, it has an enormous effect. Touch is so powerful an emotional tool that the Torah has placed special stress on where and how it can be used. This topic is beyond the scope of this work, but for our purpose, parents certainly need to be aware of the importance of harnessing the power of touch to communicate with their children.

With older children, if there is a strain in the relationship, touch must be used cautiously. It is very personal and could be considered invasive or aggressive if employed by someone to whom the child does not feel close.

Sincerity

Before speaking with anyone, take the time to feel deeply what you are about to say. This is doubly true with children.

This brings to mind the famous saying "*Devarim hayotzim min halev nichnasim el halev* — Words that come from the heart enter the heart."[30] In the same vein, when people ask me what they should speak about in a presentation, I always tell them, "Something that's important to you. Something you sincerely believe in."

Children can sense very quickly how sincere you are. This has both to do with your honesty, with how much you believe in what you are saying, and with the degree to which you are prepared to back up your words. The most eloquent words will

---

29. *Chiddushei Aggados, Berachos* 6a.

30. This phrase doesn't appear in the Talmud but seems to be an application of the *gemara* in *Berachos* 6b: "Whoever has *yiras Shamayim*, his words are heard." See *Michlol HaMa'amarim V'Hapisgamim* (Jerusalem: Mossad HaRav Kook, 1961), vol. 1, p. 502; see also *Shirah Yisrael* by Rav Moshe Ibn Ezra, p. 156, where this saying appears.

be ineffectual if the child senses that you are not really ready to stand behind your words and enforce them or that you do not really believe in what you are saying. In either case, your words will be flouted with impunity; worse, you will be considered a hypocrite in the child's eyes.

Rav Moshe Feinstein, *zt"l*,[31] explained that we must be sincere and be true models of what we want our children to be based on Hashem's demand that we be a holy nation since He is holy. Hashem is saying, so to speak, that I can demand holiness from you, because I Myself am holy.

Yes, sometimes we may fall short from what we aspire to be, but certainly we must be totally in line in our hearts, totally sincere, in what we say to our children. Otherwise, we are teaching them hypocrisy, and we are sure to eventually lose their respect. From there to losing them to the street is but a short step.

Facial expression

The *Navi* tells us that a person's facial expression is a powerful guide to the emotions that are behind his words. It says, "The face testifies against them."[32] It is no coincidence that the Hebrew word for "face," *panim*, is related to the word *penim*, "inside," for the face tells us what the person is thinking and feeling.

The Gemara teaches us that it is better to show another person "the white of your teeth" (i.e., give them a smile) than to give him a drink of milk.[33] Rav Avigdor Miller, *zt"l*, says[34] that this means that even when a person has come in from a long walk on a hot day, and he really needs a drink, a smile does more than a cold, refreshing glass of milk.

---

31. *Derash Moshe, Kedoshim*, p. 22.
32. *Yeshayahu* 3:9.
33. *Kesubos* 111b.
34. *Sha'arei Orah*, vol. 2, p. 105.

Young children are especially sensitive to our facial expressions, and they react to what they see on our faces long before they comprehend what we are saying to them. Children are emotional beings, and the sense of sight touches their emotions before they can even understand the words we're saying to them.

All this is a powerful argument for paying special attention to the nonverbal components that come with the words we utter.

It is told that Rav Yosef Chaim Sonnenfeld, *zt"l*, avoided using a telephone for important conversations. The nonverbal parts of speech that we have mentioned are far more powerful in person than over the phone.

Other factors

In addition to the five nonverbal elements just mentioned, there are other factors that can affect the success or failure of your communication with your child. They are also nonverbal and deeply influence how your words will be taken. For instance:

1. *Be conscious of the setting.* Our surroundings deeply affect what goes on in our heads. Just as a child is less likely to open up to a principal when he is seated on the other side of a huge mahogany desk than if the principal takes him out for pizza — or at least sits next to him on the same side of the desk — so would a parent do well to pay heed to the surroundings that he chooses when talking to a child.

Not only is the child affected by the location where the conversation is taking place; so is the parent. At home the parent is often distracted and can't give the child full or continuous attention. This lack of attention is a deep nonverbal message. When a person is given full attention, the respect he is accorded encourages him to express his feelings more freely. *If I feel respected, I feel hopeful that my words will be respected, and that encourages me to open up.*

Also, the fact that the parent went through the trouble to go to a setting more conducive to communication sends a powerful message to the child. He realizes how important he is to the parent.

Take a child out when you need to speak about something sensitive. Turn off your cell phone; even better, make sure your child sees you turn it off. He needs to see that you consider the time with him important and you don't want to be disturbed. Try to make the environment as relaxing and nonthreatening as possible. And remember, don't save these kinds of encounters only for lectures; otherwise, the child will get uneasy just at the suggestion of a "little talk" outside the home.

> A 9-year-old stole his aunt's cell phone and then denied it. His mother, who enjoyed a generally good relationship with her child, drove to a place that was quiet and green. Then she began to cry. When her son asked what was wrong, she said she was hurt that her child had lied to her. The child, in those calm and beautiful surroundings, apologized and promised never to lie again. There is no question that if there had not been a good relationship in place, the tears and the environment would not have helped, but there is also no doubt that the serene surroundings contributed to an atmosphere that fostered openness and closeness.

2. Be calm, focused — and listen! It is important to put other matters out of your mind when you are talking to your child. This helps the child to relax and open up. It also lets you to see matters with greater perspective. Thinking about stresses at work will not help you be patient as you discuss a behavioral issue with your child.

Cultivating calmness and focus also helps you be a better listener, which, ironically, is an enormous factor in good communication. *The best way to be a good conversationalist is to be a good listener first!* Listening is in itself a powerful, vital element in establishing a good relationship with a child. It is part of the effort that we make to show our children that we are trying to understand them. One of the greatest compliments that we can give our children is to make the sincere effort to understand them. Then there is a great hope that they will make the same effort.

Turning Ideas into Action▶

▶ *Find ways to show your child — nonverbally — that you have heard and respected what he said.*

Mori V'Rabi, *zt"l*, said that people treasure their own conclusions, as it says, "In his [that is, the person's own] Torah he thinks day and night."[35] In a verbal communication, the speaker is trying to convince the listener of the correctness of his idea. Many people — children included — resist agreeing with someone else.[36] Better to allow the child to come to his own conclusions through nonverbal cues. A couple of examples of nonverbal messages:

1. Ask the child about something she said to you yesterday or, better yet, some time earlier. It can be an idea the child stated or a worry or any other emotion that the child shared with you. Your remembering what she said sends a powerful nonverbal message that you hear and respect them.

2. Repeat what he shared with you and how much you enjoyed or found meaningful what he told you.

---

35. *Tehillim* 1:2. The plain meaning of the verse is "In His [Hashem's] Torah he thinks day and night."

36. The Telsher Rosh Yeshivah, Rav Yehudah Leib Bloch, *zt"l*, said in his essay *"V'Es Tzenu'im Chochmah,"* that this is why the one who answers *amen* to a blessing recited by someone else has greater merit then the one who recited the blessing. The one pronouncing the blessing is making his own statement; the one who answers *amen* is agreeing with the other's declaration.

► *Focus only on the child.*

Make sure that when your child speaks to you, you show total interest in what he is saying, and do not do anything else while the child is addressing you. The same is true when you are playing a game with the child. As tempting and as easy as it may be to do something else when, for instance, it's the child's turn in the game, resist doing anything else. For your child, the pleasure he gets from playing the game comes from the fact that he is playing with his mother or father, not the game itself.[37]

---

37. Along these lines, it's better to hire someone to tutor your son and you play with your child than to tutor your child and hire someone to play with him! Certainly it is a Torah mitzvah for you to learn with your son, but you can hire someone to be your agent if need be. You can't — I should hope — hire someone to be your child's mother or father and share the kind of intimate closeness that playing a game together generates.

Confrontations with Our Children: Why Children Fight Us and Why We Can't Avoid It

Part 1: The Roots of Chutzpah

*O*ne of life's most hurtful and frustrating experiences is fighting with our children. Often we end up being hurt by a child's chutzpah. Let us examine the source of that chutzpah. Understanding the root of the behavior will help us avoid it!

You don't have to yell

Parents sometimes complain that their children have "chutzpah." They don't do what their parents ask them to do, and they can be quite vocal in their opposition. I often hear the complaint "I have to scream at them before they obey me."

Too many parents feel forced into yelling and using other forms of intimidation to get their children to listen to them. How can we make our homes into more pleasant, more peaceful places and still get our children to do what we ask? How do we avoid confrontations without surrendering to our own children?

Before addressing this question, I would like to give an earthy, but true, definition of a child: *A child is someone who would rather die than lose.*

What does this mean and why is it so? And how does it relate to our discussion about confrontations?

Who are we anyway?

To truly understand this subject, we have to take a detour and study an important life principle:

Only an internal definition of self, unrelated to our surroundings, can be a true barometer of who we really are.

The Maharal teaches us[38] that *we cannot measure a person by comparing him to what is outside of him.* That is, according to the Mishnah, wealth, strength, and wisdom are not quantified by how much money a person has, how big his muscles are, and how much he knows, because all that is relative to his surroundings. A middle-income American tourist in Uganda may be perceived as being fabulously wealthy, and in a kindergarten any adult would be strong. Among the ignorant, even someone with a little knowledge is perceived as a scholar.

It is for this reason, the Maharal tells us, that the Mishnah uses self-based definitions for strength, wealth, and wisdom. Strength is measured by our ability to conquer ourselves: to prevail over the negative traits and attitudes that wreak havoc

---

38. *Derech Chaim*, beginning of Ch. 4.

with our lives. Wealth is relative to how happy we are with our lot; if we are satisfied with what we have, we are rich. Wisdom is defined by how much a person loves wisdom, by how much he seeks to learn from everyone, even those who are seen as his inferiors.

Similarly, the Mishnah gives us an objective way of measuring self-worth.

The measure of self-worth

The Mishnah teaches us, "Who is honored? The one who honors others."[39] We can now understand this in the light of the principle we stated above: that who we are has nothing to do with our surroundings or with what anyone else possesses. When someone has an inner, secure feeling of self-worth, he can freely give honor without fearing that his own honor will be deprecated in any way.[40] The Telsher Rosh Yeshivah, Rav Yosef Leib Bloch, *zt"l*, teaches this principle with the following beautiful example:[41]

> When a person arrives late for a meeting, and all the available chairs are occupied, who is the person most likely to give up his chair to the newcomer without being concerned about what others will think of him? Usually it's the most distinguished participant, because he feels secure and has no need to prove himself. A lesser person will not give up his place, because he is worried about how it will look to the others. He is concerned that others will think that the newcomer is more important than he is and that is why he surrendered his seat to him.

---

39. *Avos* 4:1.

40. See also Mind-Set 9, "The Great Challenge: Fulfilling My Potential," for more on measuring self-worth.

41. See Rav Bloch's essay on royalty in *Shiurei Da'as* (Tel Aviv: Netzach, 1953), p. 19, s.v. "*meluchah.*"

This concept is taken to its ultimate conclusion by the statement of our Sages that "wherever Scripture describes the greatness of HaKadosh Baruch Hu, we also find [in the same verse, a description of] His humility."[42] Here we see the essential sign of Hashem's innate greatness: He is humble. It is for this reason, says the Maharal, that wherever Hashem's greatness is described, His humility is also mentioned. Not only does this not detract from His greatness, but is, in effect, a sign that His greatness exists.

Now we can return to our discussion about children and confrontations.

"Winning" and "losing"

An internal sense of self-worth is something children generally have not yet had time to acquire. Hence they take their cues of who they are from what goes on around them.

We see this in their play. Children love all sorts of games, but they especially love competitive games. Often they become distraught and angry when it seems that they or their "side" is losing the game. Children don't want to lose. They associate losing with the idea that somehow they are less worthy or intrinsically less capable.[43] An important reality in understanding children emerges: *Children often measure themselves by what goes on around them rather than by who they really are.*

Several important ideas flow from this concept. Without a strong self-image, children are much more influenced by their surroundings. Mori V'Rabi, *zt"l*, used to say that a child is like a new immigrant who learns how the citizens of his adopted

---

42. *Megillah* 31a, citing *Devarim* 10:17–18. There the verse says that Hashem is "the great, mighty, and awesome G-d," and then right afterward it says that "He executes justice on behalf of the orphan and widow."

43. See Rav Moshe Schwab, *zt"l*, *Ma'archei Lev*, vol. 3, p. 212, and Maharal, *Derech Chaim*, on *Avos* 4:1.

country behave and then copies them. It is therefore vital to choose a proper environment for children.

The Rosh Yeshivah, *zt"l*, taught that when the Mishnah teaches that it is better to be "the tail of a lion than the head of a fox"[44] — that is, that a person will grow more from being a junior member of a strong group of scholars than the leading member of a weak group of ignoramuses — this does not refer to children. A more mature person can see the larger picture and deal with the fact that in his surroundings he is considered small and weak. For a child, however, his surroundings are his world, and he will consider himself a tail without realizing he is part of a lion!

This applies, by the way, when a parent has to choose whether his child should be one of the oldest in her grade or one of the youngest. The difference between someone who just became 4 and a child who just turned 5 is more than a year; you also have to factor in maturity, coordination, social skills, and size. Even if the child is intelligent and understands the class work, sometimes she is not yet capable of the more abstract thinking required in higher grades. The child may not be able to keep up with her more mature classmates, and a child used to success in school may well become unhappy and frustrated. There are no hard and fast rules, but generally, from my experience as a teacher, this holds true: let your child be the head of a younger grade rather than the tail of an older grade!

What does this have to do with confrontations and chutzpah?

Confrontations beget more confrontations

What often happens when a parent confronts a child is that the parent is surprised by the level of what seems to be a mindless, stubborn ("*chutzpadik*") reaction. Perhaps taking a bath or coming into the dining room when called or doing homework is important enough for the parent to issue a confrontational

---

44. *Avos* 4:15.

ultimatum ("Do...NOW!" "Get into the...or else!"). But the child has far more invested emotionally in not obeying the command than the parent has in having it obeyed. Why?

Unless the child has been emotionally broken, he will see the confrontational language the way a bull sees the cloth waving in the hands of the toreador. *Obeying the order is seen as "losing."* A challenge has been issued, and obedience is equated with defeat. So the child reacts with more energy and emotion than the parent expected (or totally ignores the order altogether).

To the parent, on the other hand, having the child take a bath or do homework right now is important, but not so important that it is worth a strenuous confrontation. Hence, more often than not, the parent backs down, surprised at the child's level of resistance. But backing down has monumental consequences. The child has learned two things. One, that he or she can win a confrontation. And two, that such victory has a very sweet taste. The next time Mommy or Tatty uses confrontational language, the child very likely will look forward to repeating his previous success. We can see this phenomenon with people addicted to the slot machine. The slot machine lets the person "win" once in a while, and (unfortunately) that occasional happy feeling can keep him in Las Vegas for a long time!

Confrontations — usually a "no-win" situation

It is for this reason that we must avoid, as much as we can, confrontational situations. We said that when children hear an order barked at them, they will either stubbornly refuse, since they are vested in "winning" the battle, or they will comply out of fear. Neither option is healthy, especially when it becomes a common occurrence. Certainly we need to let children know when a request is urgent and needs immediate compliance, but *when stern orders, meant to be obeyed immediately, become a way of life, something is very wrong.*

Parents may think they can browbeat children into doing what they want, but they are unaware of the effect that total, fearful compliance can have on a child. And if the child, as can often be expected, refuses, then the stage is set for a battle of wills. This battle has no winners. If the child succeeds in defying parental authority — that is, if the parent, having issued a stern command, backs down in the face of the child's intransigence — then the parent can be assured, as we have already mentioned, that stubborn refusals will be repeated. Even if the child is, on later occasions, forced to comply, the memory of that one "victory" will remain in the child's mind, and he will continue to defy the parents, hoping that his earlier success will be repeated.

If the parent always "wins" — that is, if the parent forces compliance by brute force or bullying — then the child will eventually become broken and have no personal initiative later in life, in addition to a poor self-image. I have seen this many times, and it is not a pretty thing to behold.

Keep in mind that confrontation does not always have to take the form of screaming; there are more subtle ways of bullying. I remember several instances where parents told their children that if the parent were not obeyed then the father would have a heart attack. Certainly a parent's health is a top priority, but matters should not have to deteriorate to the point where the threat of a parental heart attack is the only means of convincing a child to take a certain course of action.

Other negative factors

Another negative aspect of confrontation is the lesson we are teaching our children when we resort to shouting, bullying, or other confrontational tactics. We are in effect teaching them that this is a way of solving problems or getting your way.

Also, confrontations often arise when we show our child that we have caught him "red-handed." While sometimes this is necessary, often it is counterproductive in the long run. Perhaps you will have proven your point with incontrovertible evidence, but there may be long-term damage to the relationship. The child will now assume that you have a low opinion of him. This has many negative side effects, not the least of which is that the child will no longer seek to maintain a modicum of good behavior in order to maintain his reputation. This is especially true of teenagers, for whom image is so important.[45]

In short, when it comes to confrontations, here is a basic rule of thumb: Confront as infrequently as possible, but when a confrontation is inevitable, then the parent must emerge, *for the child's sake*, the "victor."

Part 2: Why Confrontations Occur

There are several reasons confrontations occur, and most often they are preventable. Let us mention some of the most prominent reasons that confrontations can become a way of life in the home.

Poor planning

When a parent hasn't planned properly, emergencies arise. This could be the result of not allotting enough time to do everything that needed doing. Or perhaps not enough thought was put into evaluating a particular task's degree of difficulty, or the amount of preparation necessary for the task was underestimated. Therefore, for example, the departure time for

---

45. This decision, whether or not to show the child that you have clear evidence of misbehavior, is a difficult one. Much of the decision will be predicated, I think, on the past relationship between the parent and child and how vital it is that the behavior be stopped as quickly as possible.

a trip arrives and things are still left to be done, or it's bed-time and many tasks need attending to. So the parent goes into "take-charge" mode, and starts issuing brisk commands. When not immediately obeyed, these commands bring in their wake confrontational language.

Perhaps the most common example of such situations is *erev Shabbos*, when there are myriad tasks to need to be done and everyone feels pressured, especially by the mother of the household. Often there is more work than can be handled on *erev Shabbos*, and children are pressed into service, sometimes against their will. This leads to tension, arguments, and recrim-inations.

It's best to tackle this problem head-on, either by beginning Shabbos preparations Thursday night or simplifying the Shab-bos meals. In extreme cases, if things have progressed so far that *erev Shabbos* routinely becomes a day of stress and confronta-tion, it would be far better, in my opinion, to have a "weekday" Shabbos; that is, one without some of the Shabbos culinary treats. Instead of screaming at the children to help out, the par-ents should explain to them that they simply cannot manage ev-erything by themselves, and they need to cut back somewhere. After a kugel-less or dessert-less Shabbos, children will probably understand that their help is needed. It must be stressed, how-ever, that this approach is not meant as a punishment, but that it is a natural outcome of the reality of the situation.

There is no doubt that children need to help prepare the home for Shabbos, just as there is no doubt that they need to participate, as responsible members of the family, in many other aspects of family life. What we are referring to here is an example of what occurs when things have gone too far, farther than they should have ever been allowed to. When that hap-pens, we need to cut back somewhere.

This cutback is done without rancor, bitterness, or anger, but it must be done. As *Mishlei* (17:1) says, "Dry bread with peace is better than a home full of meat with strife,"[46] while our Sages teach us, "Make your Shabbos as a weekday, and do not impose on people"[47] — and here, I believe, "people" can also refer to your children.[48] If *erev Shabbos* has become a day of confrontation, simplify and enter Shabbos with a smile.

Parental self-esteem

Sometimes parents feel that they must "win" lest their status in the home be undermined. These parents feel insecure and must prove that they are "boss," that for "the good of the home" everyone must show who's in charge. It becomes an emotional issue, with each side intent on "winning."

Often, as we said, the parents lose. In fact, confrontations can cause the opposite effect: rather than boosting the parents' status in the home, it may deteriorate. The truth is, *someone who needs to show that he or she is boss isn't the boss at all, and even children can sense that.*

This is but one of many reasons that a parent must build up his or her sense of self-worth.[49] The subject of how this is done is a vital one, but is not our present subject.

Poor sleep and diet

There can be no question that *when a person doesn't sleep or eat properly, his patience wears thin.* This is certain to con-

---

46. *Mishlei* 17:1.

47. *Shabbos* 118a.

48. This is certainly not the simple meaning of this statement of Chazal. There it refers to not taking charity in order to indulge in Shabbos expenses. What I am suggesting is that we can learn from this *gemara* that it is preferable to simplify rather than "impose" on our children in a confrontational manner.

49. See Rav Yosef Leib Bloch's abovementioned parable in *Shiurei Da'as.* The most important person in the room is more willing than anyone else to give up his seat. He isn't concerned about looking important, because he *is* important.

tribute to a climate that is likely to turn confrontational. Taking care of yourself physically is an intrinsic part of taking care of your family.

Disrespectful language

When people generally don't talk to each other respectfully, confrontational language becomes the norm and people dig in to defend their positions. Respectful speech between husband and wife or parent and child will go a long way toward avoiding confrontation.

Lifestyle

Sometimes a parent is overburdened with various responsibilities, in or out of the home, which create stress. This stress makes a person more needy for things to work out, and a smoothly running home becomes a vital emotional need. The reality is that in families, especially families with several younger children or a few teenagers, or both, it is the norm for things not to go smoothly. This puts the family at risk for confrontations.

If you feel that stress is an unavoidable part of your normal daily life, then you should be giving thought to which of your commitments can either be eliminated or minimized. Priorities need to be set, and some important matters may have to be put on hold for the time being (perhaps until your children have grown up). *It is far better to cut back on your commitments and allow yourself more time to be even tempered with your child than to endure the deep pain of shattered relationships.*

Part 3: When You Can't Avoid Confrontations

Now that we know why confrontations occur, and why they can be so damaging, let's examine situations when confrontation is inevitable.

The importance of a positive relationship

Every confrontation is a strain on a relationship. Though it should never be part of a child's daily fare, it is sometimes necessary or unavoidable.

Parents must be aware of a very powerful rule: Before putting strain on a relationship, it is first necessary to build, nurture, and develop the relationship in positive ways. This is true of all relationships.

First and foremost, a parent must build a strong, positive relationship with the child. That way, when there is a tight moment — and there will be tight moments — the parent will be able to give a curt command and the child will not feel put down and demeaned. He will not feel like a "loser." He or she will understand that this is a difficult moment for Mommy or Daddy and will comply with the request, mindful of the unusual urgency that the parent is displaying.

When and where do we confront our children?

It must be emphasized here that when we use the word *confrontation*, we are not talking about bitter or loud tones of voice or threats of dire consequences. We are simply talking about firmly "putting your foot down." As Mori V'Rabi, *zt"l*, put it, we must always remain "fair, firm, and friendly." With this understanding, we can present some of the most important questions that should be answered before choosing the confrontational path:

1. *Does it affect the "inner person"?* If the child's negative behavior will have an effect on his perception of self and life — that is, it will affect his character or basic ideals — then a clear and firm stand is in order. This includes lying, bullying others, or a tendency to erupt into fits of temper. These areas affect a person's chance at a successful life and must be dealt with as soon as they become evident.

2. *Is it common knowledge in the home?* Often, if a particular form of misbehavior has become public household knowledge, a parent may need to react. This is particularly true when dealing with an older child whose actions are often copied by younger siblings. Enormous care must be exercised here, since the older child will be especially sensitive to a public confrontation and go to great lengths to "win." A delicate balance must be struck between letting the younger children know that you don't approve of behavior that you consider bad for your children and that you will take steps to control it and preserving the dignity of the child in question.

One way of doing this is to give reasons for the child's misbehavior that puts him in a better light. Statements such as "It must have been a very difficult day for you to have spoken that way to me," "You probably don't know where this could lead," or "This probably wasn't your idea," can preserve a child's image while demonstrating that you disapprove.

3. *Will you — and your spouse — weather the confrontation?* Remember that adults often underestimate the lengths that children will go through in order to win a confrontation. You must be firm in your resolve, convinced of the correctness of choosing to confront. Otherwise, you will end up giving in and find yourself far worse off than if you had never initiated the confrontation.

This, of course, includes your spouse's resolve. If your husband or wife is not convinced of the correctness of your cause, or lacks the emotional fortitude to weather the difficult moments that every confrontation brings, then don't begin.

Children are experts at "divide and conquer"; they will sense your spouse's weakness and exploit it to the end. This is especially true if your child has won confrontations in the past. Then it is truly amazing how much effort he will invest in winning. After winning once, children believe firmly in their ability to win again.

4. *Is it a precedent that can change the way the home functions, or is it a temporary situation?* If the behavior is likely to repeat itself, there is more reason to put a quick stop to it. Often, however, problematic behavior is the result of a "stage" that the child is going through, or it is the result of certain environmental causes, such as the boredom of a long summer or the day after a wedding. Such events upset a child's equilibrium and cause him to act out. In that case, firm action is not called for, since the behavior will cease when the conditions that caused it are no longer a reality. The proper approach to such forms of misbehavior is to address the underlying causes for it, or else just be patient and it will disappear of its own accord. Under this category is also behavior that the child will eventually outgrow.

> A young child had seated himself in Rav Yaakov Kamenetsky's place in shul. The father was about to rebuke his child when Rav Yaakov stopped him. When the child matured, said Rav Yaakov, he would certainly not seat himself in the Rav's chair. Right now it was enough to remove the child from the Rav's seat and tell him, "We don't sit in the Rav's place."[50]

5. *Do you understand the misbehavior?* Often the reason for the misbehavior is unclear to the parents. The confrontation may eliminate the misbehavior, but if the cause is not considered, then the misbehavior will repeat itself, in the same form or another, and this will invite more confrontations. This is

---

50. See *Reb Yaakov*, p. 328.

analogous to curing pneumonia with a powerful drug, but not making sure that the home is properly heated and free of cold, windy drafts. It's important that the home be "well heated": warm and loving and draft-free.

How do you get to the bottom of the situation? Parents often ask me how to deal with a specific form of misbehavior, such as stealing or hitting a younger sibling. It's important to realize *why* the child is doing this. Often the child is just immature and the parent needs to put effort into preventing the child from doing these things until he matures. But more often, there are deeper, underlying reasons. Sometimes the child is aware of them and sometimes he isn't. When there is an ongoing, trusting, and loving relationship with the parent, the child can open up about what he is thinking and feeling and they can investigate what are the sources of the negative behavior.

Ongoing is a key word. If the bonding time between parent and child occurs only when there is a problem, the child will either refuse to open up or create difficult situations in order to get the parent to give him the time that he so craves.

Gifts, war, and, especially, prayer

I think that this chapter will have a fitting close if we apply the principle set forth by the Sfas Emes.[51] The Sfas Emes describes how Yaakov dealt with Esav. A confrontation was brewing, and Yaakov wanted to avoid it if possible. The Sfas Emes uses this event to discuss how a person should deal with his *yetzer hara*, but what he says is, I believe, equally true when dealing with children, who, as Mori V'Rabi, *zt"l*, said, are dominated by their *yetzer hara*.[52]

---

51. *Vayishlach* 5645, p. 148.

52. See the Rosh on *Nedarim* 32b, who says that the *yetzer hatov* is called a "child" because it is 13 years younger than the *yetzer hara*. This implies that children do not even acquire a *yetzer tov* until the age of 12 or 13 – see *Tzidkas HaTzaddik* 119.

The Sfas Emes notes that Yaakov employed three strata-gems. The first was *doron*, sending gifts, then he prepared for war, and, finally, he prayed.[53] We, as well, need to combat the *yetzer hara* by remembering the vast kindnesses that Hashem bestows on us. This breeds a love for Hashem: the first line of defense against the *yetzer hara*.

The second strategy that we need to employ, should these "gifts" be insufficient, is *milchamah*, war: direct confrontation.

The third weapon that Yaakov invoked — and the Sfas Emes calls this the main weapon that we have — is *tefillah*, prayer. Without Hashem's help, we stand no chance against the *yetzer hara*.

The same is true, I think, with our children. First we must draw them close, develop a positive relationship with them. Only then can we contemplate war: confrontations. But, above all, we cannot succeed at anything with our children without Hashem's blessing, without prayer.

---

53. This is in accordance with the order mentioned in the Sfas Emes; accord-ing to Rashi, prayer preceded war.

Turning Ideas into Action▶

▶ *Evaluate and assess.*

Take some quiet time, at least once a week, to assess your relationship with your child:

1. Am I developing a positive, nurturing relationship with my child? This can be through

a. spending time together, either by playing with him or just listening,

b. remembering and following up (depending on your child's age and natural desire for privacy) on previous conversations, or

c. giving the child some treat or small gift that he didn't expect.

2. Review your week in the light of your life priorities: are the things that you are investing in most the same things that reflect your dearest life priorities?

3. Make sure your schedule is not unduly crowded, especially during the time that you spend with your children, and that your time with them finds you in a calm, happy frame of mind.

4. Think through the previous week's confrontations: Do I see a pattern that could have been avoided? Were they all over things that were really important to you or deeply important to the long-term welfare of your child?

5. Take time to reevaluate and understand the differences between your children: Do I understand their varying needs? Most importantly, do my children believe that I understand them?

6. Make time to plead with Hashem to

a. guide you in properly understanding your children,

b. help you find the reserves to react to them correctly and guide them on the path of Torah, and

c. protect your children from bad influences.

CHAPTER 4

Cosmic Strategies for Daily Living

Insider Knowledge: How to Fight Public Enemy Number One

K nowing the enemy is the first step in developing strategies toward victory. In this mind-set you will receive an insider's view of the antagonist that keeps us locked in battle all our lives: the yetzer hara.

The "other" side

We know that Hashem created a world of free will. This means that there will always be two sides to every question, and both will vie for our attention and consent. With everything we face, we have a choice between two voices: one an expression of Hashem's will and "another side," literally, a "sitra achra," which beckons to us.

Mori V'Rabi, *zt"l*, explained that the *sitra achra* is translated as "the other side," but really it is the *opposite* of the side of *kedushah*. *Seforno* says[1] that the power of the *sitra achra* is in deception, what is called "*dimyon*." In essence, a *dimyon* is a fake copy of the real thing.

How does this manifest itself? Primarily in two ways:

1. Hashem says keep the Torah. The *yetzer hara* claims it's too difficult, it can't be done.

2. Hashem presents and teaches truth. The *yetzer hara*, the other side, distorts truth.

The two strategies of the yetzer hara

According to the Vilna Gaon,[2] these two strategies of the *yetzer hara* were apparent very early on, in man's first encounter with the *sitra achra*: when Chavah met with the *nachash*, the snake, in Gan Eden. The Vilna Gaon sees these two classic arguments of the *sitra achra* being presented in the snake's discussion with Chavah.

When attempting to persuade Chavah to eat the forbidden fruit, the snake told her:

1. You can't eat from *any* of the trees of the Garden[3] (although the command was only regarding the tree of knowledge); that is, it's impossible to keep Hashem's commandments.

2. You will not die if you eat of the tree;[4] a distortion of the truth.

It is important to recognize that our *yetzer* constantly uses these two distinct and different strategies against us:

1. When you know the action is wrong, but you feel it's too hard to refrain from doing it; that it's impossible to keep the

---

1. On *Bereishis* 3:1.

2. *Aderes Eliyahu, Bereishis* 3:1–3.

3. *Bereishis* 3:1.

4. Ibid. 3:4.

Torah. This, I believe, is a form of the *yetzer hamisgaber* mentioned in the Gemara.[5]

2. When the *yetzer* distorts truth so you don't even know that anything is wrong with what you're doing. This is sometimes called the *yetzer hamischadeish*, a "new" *yetzer*, where you come across something new and whether it is true or false — whether or not it is a product of the *yetzer hara* — is as yet unclear.[6]

We see these two different aspects of the *yetzer hara* in the two voices that spoke to the Jews who came to the United States at the end of the 19th century and the beginning of the 20th. Shabbos observance was deemed either "too hard"; that was the *yetzer hamisgaber* talking. Or they declared, "America is different, it's not a place for Old World traditions"; that was the voice of the *yetzer hamischadeish*.

Defending ourselves

The *yetzer hara* has formidable strategies, but our counter-strategies are just as formidable. The defense against the first claim is *ahavas Hashem*, love of Hashem. *When you love someone, even difficult things seem easy.* When our *ahavas Hashem* is firmly rooted within us, we realize that the *yetzer's* claim is false and that doing Hashem's will really isn't difficult. In fact, it's the opposite of difficult, because doing what's right gives us the key to meaning and, as a result, the key to happiness.[7]

The second claim of the *yetzer hara* is an exact distortion of the truth: what seems to be a mitzvah is really an *aveirah*. To counter this we need to ponder: What does Hashem have to say about this? This is an outgrowth of *yiras Hashem:* realizing

---

5. *Succah* 52a.

6. Ibid.

7. Happiness comes from fulfilling our purpose and having meaning in our lives. See the first section of this book, "The Happiness Mind-Set."

that Hashem sees everything and has an opinion about it.[8] In developing our awe of Hashem, we learn to use our minds and become objective enough to know Hashem's will, and see through the distortions that the *yetzer* presents us.

> Mori V'Rabi, *zt"l*, related that when he was young, socialism was taking the world by storm, preaching social fairness and wealth. It was clear that this wasn't a Torah "ism," but many *ehrliche* Jews were swept away by it, convinced that it was in keeping with Torah values.
>
> Mori V'Rabi gave these new ideas much thought and examined it from a Torah perspective. He considered that the Socialist Manifesto defended the rights of the workers of the world, yet there was no mention of their obligations, such as devoting a full, honest day's work to their employers.
>
> He also noted that the Torah accords the Jewish master and his servant a different set of responsibilities. If there was one pillow in the house, the servant got it, not the master, but the servant had to put in a full day of honest work. Mori V'Rabi concluded that socialism could never reflect Torah ideals since its basic tenet was against Torah. The Torah is fair, but not everyone is equal; everyone has different responsibilities and receives what they need accordingly.
>
> Mori V'Rabi used his G-d-given intellect and, with *yiras Hashem*, was able to see through the distortions of socialism.

Sometimes we need a little help to see the truth and have to seek advice from those who have the requisite level of *yiras Hashem*.

---

8. See Rav Avigdor Miller, *zt"l*, *Sha'arei Orah*, vol. 2, p. 12.

Turning Ideas into Action ▶

▶ *Counterstrategies for the yetzer hara's claim that keeping the Torah is too hard:*

▶ *Break it down.*

There are things we would love to do, but we think that they are too difficult for us. Break them down into doable tasks, taking just one small step at a time that you can do for a relatively short period of time. When we manage to do something that we had originally thought would be too hard for us, we look at ourselves differently. (In general, we raise our self-esteem when we achieve something difficult, something we didn't think we could manage to do.) Then, the next time, the *yetzer hara* will have a harder time telling us that something is too difficult. At the very least, you can respond by saying that doing what's right is temporarily within reach, and for the next few days, at least, I can manage to live by the Torah's demands and earn a better life even in this world.

Here are some suggestions for making difficult things more manageable in several important areas in life: "It must be emphasized that these exercises must be done one at a time. You can rotate them, that is, do one for a half a week and then do another. Or else, if you feel you are benefitting from a specific exercise, keep doing it for as long as you are getting something out of it. The exercises on this page can take years but they will yield a huge benefit. Remember, take slow but steady steps.

▶ *Physical health:*

Stay away from unhealthy food for two or three days. The Torah mandates that we take care of our bodies. It may be too hard to consider a complete break from unhealthy foods, but for a few days it is doable with a little effort. After two or three days go by without your succumbing to foods that are bad for you, you will feel differently about yourself.

▶ *Spiritual health:*

Resolve, for just a few days, to say the first berachah of Birkas HaMazon from a siddur. Before you start, remember that only a short while before you were hungry, and now you are no longer hungry. Pause for a moment and feel grateful for this.

▶ *Emotional health:*

Maintain a positive mind-set. (1) Decide that for the next three days you will enter your home at the end of the day in an appreciative frame of mind. This can be a sense of gratitude for something big, such as being married or enjoying good health or for "just" having a place to come home to. (2) Resolve to see even a small detail of what's right in your home and feel grateful for it. It can even be for the fact that you have a comfortable pillow to lay your head on. (3) If you are a mother, make up your mind that for the next few days you will try to make your children feel that you are really happy to see them when they come through the door after school and that you genuinely want to hear about their day.

Counterstrategies for the yetzer hara's distortion of truth:

▶ ***Think things through.***

Once a day, resolve to think a matter through again without coming to a quick conclusion. On second thought, things may look different. The great Rav Yechezkel Abramsky, *zt"l*, a world-class Torah genius, would think through a class that he needed to teach *eight times* before presenting it, because after a number of times that something is examined, new ideas and perspectives often come to light.[9]

▶ ***Talk it over.***

Discuss a thought that you had with someone else to see if you've missed something, or if you misread or misunderstood someone or something. This person need not be someone older or wiser than you, just someone with a different, fresher perspective. Your drive for truth will be enhanced by this, because you will often see that indeed you may have missed something.

▶ ***Turn to Torah study.***

When you exert yourself to seek truth, you will be better able to see through the lies of the *yetzer hara*. There is no question that proper study of Torah, especially with a learning partner, is one of the greatest ways of honing our appreciation for truth. An ongoing and sincere exposure to Torah and the effort invested in seeking the truth in the Torah we study will in and of itself encourage the pursuit of truth and enhance the ability to see through falsehood.[10]

---

9. See Rav Chaim Friedlander, *Sifsei Chaim, Middos*, vol. 2, p. 61.

10. When Rav Aharon Kotler, *zt"l*, was shown the design for the yeshivah's new stationery, he rejected it. Why? At the top of the stationery was an artist's rendition of the yeshivah building. The artist had added a few trees, which weren't actually there, to enhance the drawing. Rav Aharon noticed this and rejected the proposed design saying, "I hate *sheker* (falsehood)!"

Connecting to Happiness

A lone in a pagan world, Avraham Avinu looked above him
and discovered Hashem. How did he do it? And how can we
follow our forefather's path?

Hopelessness and prophecy

There are two ways that a person can come to *emunah*, to
faith in Hashem. We see both ways in the life of the first man
of true *emunah*, Avraham Avinu:

1. *A person can understand the hopelessness and decadence of
what is going on around him and realize that this cannot be the
right way.* This should compel him to seek out Hashem.

To illustrate this manner of finding Hashem, the Shem
MiShmuel[11] cites the famous midrash that relates a conversation between Nimrod and Avraham.[12] In that dialogue, Avraham

---

11. *Lech Lecha*, p. 98.
12. See *Bereishis Rabbah* 38:13.

rejected each "god" because there was something greater: water puts out fire, so it's senseless to worship fire. The cloud carries the water, so why bow down to water? The wind carries the cloud and man carries the wind within him, and so it went. This was not discovery of God in the positive sense, just a rejection of what was wrong or inferior. It is a more limited knowledge of Hashem's existence, but a necessary first step.

The second path is more positive:

2. *A person can gain a clear picture of Hashem Himself through prophecy.*

Two stages

These two paths to faith are reflected in the two stages of Avraham's life:

1. the era when he discovered Hashem's existence, ending with Nimrod throwing him into the fiery furnace, and

2. the era beginning when Hashem appeared to him and commanded him to leave his home.

In the first part of his life, Avraham knew that there was a Creator — that there had to be a Higher Being Who had created all that he saw around him — and Avraham was ready to die for Him. But Who this Creator was, he did not know. Not, that is, until Hashem appeared to him with the words "*Lech lecha* — Go!"

These two paths of *emunah* reflect two different aspects of Hashem's relationship with us: the trait of Divine retribution and the trait of Divine kindness. The two eras of Avraham's life and these two phases of *emunah* are also reflected in two different words: *kadosh*, holy, and *baruch*, blessed.

Before Hashem appeared to him, Avraham taught the world that there is a God Who is Holy; it was only later that Avraham showed the world that God is also Blessed. *Kadosh*, holy, refers to a God Who is involved in the world and Who punishes evildoers. *Baruch*, blessed, shows us the deeper reality of Hashem, the God Who is full of Divine goodness.

The Gra explains[13] that we call Hashem "HaKadosh Baruch Hu," referring to the two ways that we see Hashem in this world. "*Kadosh*" refers to the One Who brings judgment to the world and causes us to fear him; "*baruch*" refers to Hashem's trait of Divine goodness. The Gra, however, does not discuss why "*kadosh*" precedes "*baruch*," why we do not call Him "HaBaruch Kodesh Hu," where the "*baruch*," the Divine goodness, comes first.

I heard that the reason that "*kadosh*" comes first is because first the trait of Divine retribution was manifest in the world. Adam and Chavah, Kayin, the generations of the flood and the tower all tasted Hashem's trait of Divine justice. But with Avraham came Hashem's promise that the world would also see Hashem's Divine goodness: "*V'heyeh berachah* — And you will be a blessing."[14]

In addition, *kadosh*, the trait of Divine retribution, precedes *baruch*, Hashem's goodness, because it is easier to see Hashem's presence when things go wrong for us, when we naturally turn to Him for help. When we enjoy good fortune, we tend to forget Hashem.

Avraham knew that there was a Creator, and he was ready to die for Him, because he knew that there was something wrong with worshiping any of the world's creations. But Who this Creator was he did not know until Hashem appeared to him. Only after Hashem appeared to him could he teach the world that the Creator is *baruch*, full of Divine goodness.

This is not to say that we can't see the kindness of Hashem in the world without prophecy. It's just that this higher level of understanding Hashem first came to Avraham as a prophetic

---

13. *Siddur HaGra*, s.v. "*v'hi she'amdah…v'HaKadosh Baruch Hu matzileinu mi-yadam.*"

14. *Bereishis* 12:2. This is based on an idea I heard from Rav Shlomo Brevda, zt"l.

vision, while the first level of understanding Hashem came from the efforts of Avraham's inquiring mind.

Bringing it into our lives

How do we, in our own lives, ensure that we see Hashem's Hand, particularly when our lives are tranquil, when we are not facing any crisis or suffering to send us racing to our *sifrei Tehillim*?

One useful exercise that I recommend is to take one of the morning blessings and focus on it throughout the day. We are enjoined by Chazal to say thank you for being able to see, for being able to walk, for being able to use a bathroom. If not for our great teachers of long ago, we would never even notice these gifts, because they are constants in our lives. Anyone who has ever walked with crutches remembers that first day when he was able to walk on his own again, when he no longer had to decide, *Do I really need to walk down these stairs?* This is how we want to feel about these gifts *every single day*.

Another way of enhancing appreciation of the good Hashem bestows is to "freeze the moment" when we experience some special good fortune. Try to memorize the moment by harnessing all of your senses. Was it light or dark, cold or hot? What did the surroundings look like? Who was with you?

When you recall a moment in such a way, rather than merely remembering that something good happened to you, you can actually relive the moment and regain a renewed appreciation of the goodness that Hashem has showered upon you.

One more way to appreciate our everyday blessings: seeing someone else's distress and contrasting it with our own fortune. We should, of course, empathize and feel for their sorrow, but at the same time it should help us appreciate the "regular" things we possess, whether it is our health, our family, or our livelihood.

Turning Ideas into Action ▶

▶ *Focus on one blessing.*

The value of an act or a mind-set is enhanced by repetition. As discussed above, focusing on one of the morning *berachos* can make a deep impression and help us notice our good fortune in everyday happenings. But don't stop at one day; take one of the *berachos* that we say daily and focus on it for as long as it is making an impression on you. *This can go on for months or even years.* The longer the *berachah* continues to affect you, the deeper and more permanent the effect will be.

▶ *Focus on one sentence of one prayer.*

The same exercise can be applied to a sentence from the daily prayers. For instance, the words "*Mizmor shir chanukas habayis l'David*" state that David HaMelech wrote a song for the inauguration of the Beis HaMikdash. Rav Avigdor Miller, *zt"l*, taught an immensely important and powerful lesson from this seemingly simple introductory *pasuk*. David knew that he could not build the Beis HaMikdash — he had been told so by Nasan HaNavi[15] — but this did not stop him from preparing the inaugural song. A person always does what he can! If you can't build the Beis HaMikdash, don't let that paralyze you. Keep going and do whatever you can

---

15. *Shmuel* II, Ch. 7.

— and that's a lot! If consistently, at least daily, repeated, this idea will give you a fuller, more meaningful, and happier life. You can do this with any sentence of the *tefillos* that speaks to you: focus on the idea and repeat it to yourself daily until it makes a deep impression on you.

Learn to Be Free: No Fear

The French Revolution heralded the age of liberty and freedom but was soon followed by beheadings and anarchy. The Declaration of Independence claimed the human right of life and liberty, but that didn't include blacks or women. Does freedom ring in today's society — a society manipulated by the media and driven by the constraints of nonstop workdays? Did Hashem take us out of Egypt to be free only on weekends?

What it means to be free

There is no such thing as a truly free person in the purely literal sense. We all have our limitations, our foibles and weaknesses. Is a multimillionaire, with all his choices, really free?

Rav Yitzchok Berkowitz, *shlita*, tells of a multimillionaire who visited Aish HaTorah. He was afraid to enter the elevator because he suffered from a phobia. Is that a free person?

President Obama, who arguably wields more power than anyone else in the world, had to fight for the right to send his personal e-mails, and he can't take a simple stroll down the street. Is that freedom?

Freedom then can't be defined as the ability to do whatever you want to do. No one truly has that kind of freedom. Even if, hypothetically, a person had such freedom, it would not be beneficial to him; unbridled freedom has been the downfall and ruin of societies and individuals since time immemorial.

Freedom, rather, should be defined as the ability to do what's right without fear. It is the ability to be unafraid of external situations and hence to be able to concentrate on getting things done, and being sure that they are the right things to do. This freedom can be achieved only by understanding and internalizing a couple of factors:

1. *The awareness that no one can truly control me.* This is because the essential me is not under the control of anyone else. Another person can take away my liberty, but not my freedom: my reactions, and how I choose to view my situation, belong only to me.

2. *The awareness that there is a higher Being to Whom, in the final analysis, everyone is answerable.* This higher Being, Hashem, is involved in my life, and I am ultimately accountable solely to Him. His evaluation of my actions has a far greater impact on my long-term well-being — that is, for eternity — than any human opinion.

It is when I internalize these truths that I become truly free. When I am not worried about what a boss — or, for that matter, anyone else — thinks of me, then I am free to do what's right.

Free — and humble

True freedom and deep humility are closely linked. A truly humble person can take on anyone, because he knows that his strength is not his own, and that it is only Hashem Who is in control of the outcome.

I was privileged to meet Rav Lazer Nannes, *zt"l*, who authored *Subbota*, an autobiographical account of his 20 years in Siberia, under the pen name Avraham Netzach. He related that when he was being interrogated by the Soviet secret police, he saw the image of his father saying, "Never fear them, for they can do nothing to you." When I came to know Rav Nannes in his later years (he lived until the age of 100), he remained fearless, never even locking his door at night.

Freedom — and hashgachah pratis

Ma'archei Lev[16] defines freedom as a function of *hashgachah pratis*: since Hashem is in complete control, there is nothing to worry about. It is for this reason that the Ten Commandments begin with a reference to Hashem, Who took us out of Egypt. Belief in a Creator isn't enough to give us peace of mind. It's the knowledge that the Creator is still in touch with His creations that gives us our freedom.

This is why the Exodus, the foundation of Judaism, is the key to our freedom as a nation. The Exodus is a clear example of Divine intervention: Hashem was in complete control, and therefore there was nothing to worry about. Thus, the Exodus became the paradigm for the only true freedom people can experience: the freedom to do what's right, without fearing what others will do.

---

16. Vol. 3, pp. 160–61, by Rav Moshe Schwab, *zt"l*.

▶ *Clarify your priorities and resolve to live by them.*

When you know your priorities, you are less likely to allow external situations to prevent you from doing what's right:

1. First, take time to make a list of life priorities. The higher the priority, the less someone should be able to coerce you into contravening them.

2. Next, take time to reflect on why these priorities are so important to you. The clearer this is to you, the more powerful will be your resolve to preserve them. This should be done only with one priority at a time; it can take a long time to internalize the importance of each one.

3. Take time to reflect on the fact that you live in a country that allows you to live a life according to your priorities. This freedom obligates you to feel grateful that you live in such a country and places an added responsibility on you to actualize these priorities in your life.

Preparing for Shabbos: Keep It Holy

S *habbos is called "mei'ein Olam Haba," a taste of the Next*
World. It's something special, holy, unique, and spiritual. At
least, that's the way it should be... Is there anything we can
do to make our Shabbos closer to Heaven than to cholent, kugel,
and an afternoon nap?

Four steps to a meaningful Shabbos

Shabbos is a time for atonement and a time for renewal.[17] It
is intrinsically holy. It's interesting that we begin our Shabbos
tefillos with *Kabbalas Shabbos* even though Shabbos does not
need us to accept it to make it holy.

---

17. See *Shabbos* 119b and Rav Shimshon Pincus, *Shabbos Malchusah*, pp.
113–17.

Though Shabbos has its own greatness in and of itself, our ability to access that greatness, to truly tap into Shabbos's enormous spiritual powers, is up to us. That is what we are expressing when we say *Kabbalas Shabbos*. The more effort we put into Shabbos preparations, the more we will be able to benefit from Shabbos itself. *We get what we prepare ourselves for.*

There is a four-step formula we can use to prepare for Shabbos. By following these four steps, we attain the peace of mind so necessary for accessing the holiness of Shabbos:

1. *Histapkus* — we find satisfaction in what we have. As Shabbos approaches, we stop working and declare that whatever we have is enough; Hashem has given us all that we need.

2. Humility — we reflect on the bounty that we have, recognize all the good things we've been blessed with, and understand that they come from Hashem.

3. We stop working in order to utilize Shabbos for Torah learning.

4. We take time away from the everyday world to reaffirm and renew our commitment to a life of meaning and direction.

These steps build upon each other: When we realize that whatever we have should give us joy and that nothing is automatically coming to us (*histapkus*), then we can humble ourselves before Hashem. That allows us to commit ourselves to Torah study, which sensitizes us to what is important in life and helps us live a life of meaning and serenity.

The day of peace, the taste of the Next World

Shabbos is called the "day of peace,"[18] and the Next World is called "*yom shekulo Shabbos*," a day that is entirely Shabbos.[19]

---

18. *Sfas Emes, Ki Sissa* 5648.
19. Rav Yerucham Levovitz, *Da'as Chochmah U'Mussar* (Jerusalem, 1972), vol. 3, p. 206.

The definition of *"peace"* is *when each thing finds its proper place within the whole.* There are no contradictions in the Next World, and everything is in its place. It is entirely Shabbos — entirely peace.

The Shabbos candles represent this peace, because they light up the house, allowing us to see everything as a whole, as a totality, while in darkness everything is separate and diverse, not part of a unified whole. This, too, was the function of Yerushalayim, the "City of Peace," where the tribes, different as they were, could find their place within the whole, as it says, "The built-up Jerusalem is like a city that is united together."[20]

Rav Shlomo Wolbe, *z"l*, says[21] that peace by definition means the bridging of differences. This does not mean that I have to "surrender" and become you, or that you have to become me; we remain ourselves, we maintain our special uniqueness, which we blend into parts of a greater whole. When differences are reconciled, we have peace.

This is the harmony that can never be completely achieved until the Next World — the peace that we can "taste" on Shabbos. The reason that Shabbos is conducive to this is that it is a day when we stop and acknowledge that Hashem is in benevolent control of the world and of our lives. This leaves our minds and hearts free to focus on our loved ones and to reconnect to them. Because we feel calm and loving, our children feel a sense of acceptance and that they have a secure place in our hearts.

On Shabbos we can "taste" peace: we can stop and appreciate the good things we have in life; we can take the time to listen to our loved ones, hear and see their concerns, appreciate them. On Shabbos we can connect with and, yes, play with our children and take a careful look at where they are holding. Was their week meaningful or frustrating? Are they optimistic or

---

20. *Tehillim* 122:3. See *Talmud Yerushalmi, Chagigah* 3:6, which says that Yerushalayim was the city were all Jews became *"chaveirim,"* trusted friends, to each other.
21. *Alei Shur*, vol. 1, p. 257.

pessimistic about the coming week? Is there some Torah truth we can share to boost their *neshamos* — and ours?

Avi Shulman, in his book *Thoughts to Build On*,[22] wrote that his father never made an appointment on Friday afternoon, even on long Friday afternoons, even nearby. He was preparing himself to accept Shabbos and take a break from weekday concerns, so that when Shabbos came he would be calm and ready to truly enjoy the peace of Shabbos. Likewise, I know someone who "hands the keys back to Hashem" on Friday night as he sings *Shalom Aleichem*. He consciously lets go of the stress of the week and lets himself feel the happiness of knowing that Hashem runs the world.

You, too, can make the most of your Shabbos: *it's time to let Hashem run the world and experience the joy of just being taken care of.*

---

22. Published by Artscroll / Mesorah, 2009.

Turning Ideas into Action ▶

▶ *Think.*

When you wake up on Friday morning, resolve that the day will pass without too much tension, so that the children will also look forward to the coming Shabbos.

▶ *Plan.*

Arrange for each child to have some share in the Shabbos preparations, not because you need their help, but because you want them to feel that Shabbos is theirs as well.

▶ *Appreciate.*

If you're going to be a guest at someone else's home for Shabbos, resolve to notice the blessing that Shabbos gives to a family and appreciate the gift of Shabbos that Hashem gave to the Jewish people.

▶ *Express.*

Close to the arrival of Shabbos, verbally accept Shabbos upon yourself. Although this is actually a halachic requirement, here it is intended as a concrete expression of your Shabbos preparations and your appreciation of its gifts.

Fighting the Fight:
The Struggles of the
Jewish People

The Jewish community in Eretz Yisrael seems to be locked in a never-ending struggle with its Arab neighbors. Why is peace in the Middle East as elusive a dream as ever? Why haven't our neighbors accepted our right to exist?

This is not a new struggle. For centuries, the non-Jewish world denied the Jewish people their dignity, at times their right to life itself. Even today we are confronted by the ugliness of anti-Semitism, often among those who call themselves "enlightened liberals." On a personal level, we sometimes hear of righteous individuals who have to struggle all their lives. Why?

Our unique existence in this world

The truth is, the Jewish people should have no place in this world. In the natural way of things, we should never have existed at all; our foremothers were barren. For this reason, *the Jew's existence is different from that of all others*. The Jewish people's existence is supernatural; it is in Hashem's hands. When they follow Hashem's will, they are on a higher plane than anything else in the world. They are elevated above nature and continue to exist despite adversity. But if, *chas v'shalom*, they don't follow His will, Hashem leaves them to the rule of nature. Since they should not have existed, they are vulnerable to their enemies.

Haman's advisers were referring to this when they told Haman that the Jews are either like the dirt or the stars; that is, either beneath or above the earth.[23] This is why Rabbi Yochanan ben Zakkai rejoiced over the fact that the Jew who does not follow Hashem's will is lower than an animal.[24] Why would he rejoice? Because the Jew has an unnatural existence: we are Hashem's people, and we can exist only when we follow His ways. When we don't, we are subject to nature and descend to a lower level than an animal.

Rav Tzadok HaKohen says[25] that since the Jewish people have no place in this world — since they never should have existed here at all — they are similar to Hashem, Who has no place in the world (but rather, the world is in His place).

The unending struggle

Because the Jews have no natural place in this world, *the Jewish people must fight for everything in this world*, beginning

---

23. *Rashi, Esther* 6:13.
24. *Kesubos* 66b.
25. *Kometz HaMinchah* 2:10; see also the Gra's commentary on *Esther* 6:13.

with their entry into Eretz Yisrael, when they had to fight the Canaanite kingdoms for their rightful inheritance.[26]

This relentless struggle characterizes both the group and the individual. Like *Klal Yisrael,* the righteous Jew, the *tzaddik,* must fight; he must conquer the innate contradictions that exist in our world. This makes his path very difficult and very painful; painful, but ultimately rewarding, because *it is the nature of a person to find satisfaction from that which comes with difficulty.*[27]

The nation that inherited the Land of Canaan first had to endure Egyptian servitude. Esav was unwilling to pay the price, he couldn't face the struggle, and therefore he could not inherit Eretz Yisrael.[28] Our Matriarchs, in contrast, were barren, because Hashem knew that their fulfillment would come only through adversity and the need to pray. They withstood their trials and fulfilled their potential.

It is a good sign when we see a need to fight, a need to struggle. Only the wicked, the *rasha,* no longer struggles, because he has already lost the fight; he's surrendered to his *yetzer hara.* The *tzaddik* struggles and struggles and never gives up: "The *tzaddik* falls seven times [i.e., many times] and gets back up."[29] That is a sign of health and eventual victory.[30]

---

26. Rav Tzadok HaKohen, *Kometz HaMinchah* 2:10. This is why, explains Rav Tzadok, the Torah records that the Canaanites conquered the lands that belonged to the sons of Shem (see *Bereishis* 12:11). Even though the Torah doesn't usually record wars, it was recorded there to teach this lesson. The sons of Shem could have remained in Eretz Yisrael and the Jewish people would have entered the land without a fight since they were family; the Jews were also descendants of Shem. But instead the Jewish people had to earn Eretz Yisrael and fight for it.

27. See Mind-Set 1, "Happiness: It's Not Easy!"

28. *Rashi, Bereishis* 36:7.

29. *Mishlei* 24:16.

30. See Mind-Set 1 for a variation of this idea.

Getting the right balance

While it is not something most people are looking for, it's important to remember that struggle is vital to growth. But, as with most spiritual endeavors, balance is essential.

In the physical world, exercise is beneficial to health when carefully balanced. Too little and too easy doesn't build up the muscles; too much can result in pain and injury. Similarly, Rav Eliyahu Dessler taught that physical health is "a proper blend of all the physical properties according to their nature..." The body must be in balance in order to be healthy.[31] The same is true in the spiritual world. In order to have productive and meaningful lives, we must face struggles and overcome them; we must make a great effort to advance. But just as we must be careful not to overdo physical exercise, to build up our muscles by slow and steady stages, so must we progress step-by-step in our spiritual growth.[32]

> A cardiologist I know learned the entire tractate of *Berachos* by heart. This achievement, impressive as it is, is even greater because he can recite the *masechta* by heart — *backward*. He can also tell you the basic points that are dealt with on each page of the tractate, starting with the bottom of page 64a and continuing backward. It goes without saying that this man is both persistent and consistent, but what really needs noting is that he did it *one page at a time*, reviewing from the first page cumulatively. That is, he consistently reviewed the pages over and over from the first page of the *masechta*. He didn't stress himself out, he was calm, and he just kept going. And he's still at it!

---

31. See *Michtav MeEliyahu*, vol. 4, p. 251, and *Sefer HaYashar* of Rabbeinu Tam, beginning of Gate 7.

32. See the Gra's commentary on *Mishlei* 19:3 for one of many sources for this.

Another person I know developed the trait of feeling gratitude and going through life without undue stress by feeling grateful for the "simple" gifts that he enjoys. He makes note of these gifts while reciting his morning blessings, in which we thank Hashem for such basics as being able to walk, being able to see, and having shoes. When something goes wrong during his day, he has habituated himself to see the day in context, and renew his gratitude for the most basic gifts of his life. Reaching such a level takes time, but since it was done gradually it became a habit, and now he can access the emotion of gratitude without stress.

In this world of struggles, we must always remember not to let a setback throw us off. Sometimes we need to regroup, but we must never surrender.

Turning Ideas into Action ▶

▶ *Take the long view.*

When faced with a situation where things aren't working out, take a moment to realize that mistakes and frustrations are a part of life. If the situation reflects a miscalculation or some other mistake on your part, resolve to learn from the mistake.

▶ *Don't let a setback push you down.*

When you have failed, have in mind the following important points:

1. A perfectionist is someone who can't separate how good he is from how well he does. He feels, wrongly, that he is as good as his actions, and he constantly depends on a perfect performance to feel self-worth. Instead, realize that a failure is an opportunity to be better prepared for the future, as Chazal teach us, "A man does not fully understand the words of Torah unless he has first stumbled in them."[33]

2. Try to recall past mistakes. You'll see that they were never as fateful or harmful as you thought they would be. Keep a record of these memories, and eventually you'll realize, even in the throes of another error, that things will not be as tragic as they seem to portend.

---

33. *Gittin* 43a.

3. Often we react less emotionally to others' mistakes; other people don't need to be as perfect as we are, and at any rate their mistakes affect us less. If the person making the mistake is a close family member, especially a spouse, resolve to remember, when it happens, that they feel badly enough as it is, and they need our support and encouragement. This is a reflection of an important rule: *we can think about how we feel or we can think about how the other person feels, but we can't do both at the same time.* We need to habituate ourselves to first focus on where the other person is emotionally, especially when the other person is a loved one. Only then can we access our own feelings, which are usually much more controlled once we have felt the other person's emotional reality.

Seeking Truth through Giving: Western Culture, Torah Values, and Our Lives

*R*eading or listening to the news often leaves us with the distinct impression that we are living in an immoral, decadent society. How can we protect our families and ourselves? What do we need to do to remain strong at a time when the world is weak spiritually, when we are surrounded by a terrible environment?

Standing against the world — the test of our times

The Torah, which has the answers to all our questions, discusses another society whose morality was on the verge of collapse: the generation of the flood. Let us take a close look at how Noach, surrounded by the depraved society that would be destroyed in the deluge, succeeded in protecting himself.

The Alter of Novardok, Rav Yosef Yozel Horowitz, zt"l, says[34] that the time of Noach marks the second era in the world's history, coming after the era of Adam, the first man, and before the era of Avraham. The generations who lived after Adam couldn't cope with the battle that they were forced to fight with the yetzer hara, which became part and parcel of them after the sin, and they consistently failed.[35] Noach was the first to merit the Divine help necessary to overcome this internal battle. The reason for this, says the Alter of Novardok, is because Noach did whatever he could do himself with all his might. Hashem helped him with the rest. And, unlike Avraham, he needed that help.

The first mind–set: Do your best

This is our first lesson: a person is expected to do his best. When we live in a world full of sin and impurity, we need to do our best to repel society's influences. We need to put much effort and thought into this formidable task, and then we are promised that Hashem will help us. This personal "best" continues to grow greater, until a person looks at himself and can't believe how far he has come.

Mori V'Rabi, zt"l, pointed out that there was enormous siyatta diShmaya, Divine help from Hashem, in the difficult days after World War II. The surviving remnant did what they could despite the odds, and with incredible help from Heaven people

---

34. Madreigas HaAdam, "Tekufas HaOlam."

35. Until Adam ate from the tree of knowledge, the yetzer hara was an external force. After his sin, it became part of him and affected his judgment in a more internal way. For a deeper, more detailed explanation of this point, see Michtav MeEliyahu, vol. 2, on Parashas Bereishis.

accomplished in small amounts of time what took much longer before the war.[36]

When expounding on this idea, Mori V'Rabi, *zt"l*, would paraphrase the Gemara that states that Rabbi Dosa ben Hyrkanos called Rabbi Akiva "a fast grower." His words were a play on the simple meaning of the blessing that Rabbi Dosa conferred upon Rabbi Akiva when he entered his home: "*Yirbu kamoscha b'Yisrael*," which literally means, "There should be many like you among Israel."[37] *Yirbu* in Aramaic means both "multiply" and "grow." Rabbi Akiva grew to greatness quickly, since he began learning only when he was 40 years old; Rabbi Dosa implied that there should be many "fast growers" like him among the Jewish people.

So, too, said Mori V'Rabi, *zt"l*, after World War II there was a period of "fast growing" for the Jewish people. It was the result of a combination of great effort on their part and incredible *siyatta diShmaya*.

The second mind-set: Figure it out!

A *Ramban* at the beginning of *Parashas Noach*[38] states that even though no prophet came to warn the generation of the flood not to steal, they were still punished for that sin. They were expected to figure out for themselves that stealing is wrong.

Living in decadent times does not give us an excuse to be decadent ourselves; we have to figure out how to live pure lives in impure societies. It's hard, but not impossible. Remember,

---

36. I heard this from Mori V'Rabi, *zt"l*, himself and also in his name from Rav Elya Yurkansky, *zt"l*, one of my great teachers at the Mirrer Yeshivah in Brooklyn, New York.

37. *Yevamos* 16a.

38. *Ramban* on *Bereishis* 6:13.

we were each given a pure and holy *neshamah* and an innate understanding of right and wrong.

Discovering more mind–sets from the secret of Noach's greatness

We can find still more "mind-sets" to help us deal with the outside world if we examine the composition of Noach's greatness. The Alter of Novardok cites a difference of opinion among Chazal as to whether Noach would have been even greater than he was had he lived in Avraham Avinu's time, or if he would not have been as great if he'd lived in that era. The two different answers to that question revolve around what, indeed, made Noach so great.

The first opinion says that *Noach became great because of his relentless search for the truth*. In the time of Avraham, he would have had less opposition, and he could have put even more energy into this search and become even greater.[39]

The second opinion says that *Noach became so great because he saw how terrible the world around him was, and this spurred him to make a greater effort*. In Avraham Avinu's time, when the world was not on such a low level, Noach would not have been forced to exercise those spiritual muscles in quite the same way. Thus, he would not have been as great as he was.

Actually, these two reasons parallel the two aforementioned mind-sets. The first reason for Noach's greatness was his unwillingness to give up; he did the best he could no matter the

---

39. This is similar to the reason that Rav Aharon Kotler, *zt"l*, gave for why Sarah insisted that Yishmael be driven away. It wasn't that he would defile Yitzchak, but that the effort that Yitzchak would need to repel the bad influence would hamper him in his efforts to become as great as he could. Indeed, Rav Avigdor Miller, *zt"l*, says that the reason that Sarah was greater than Avraham in prophecy was because Avraham had to ward off a noxious environment in order to teach others. Sarah, on the other hand, stayed at home, and only the most refined women came to see her.

circumstances. The worse the circumstances, the greater the merit of the person unwilling to give up. But even in Avraham's time, Noach would have put in a great effort. No matter what, he would have done his best.

The second reason seems to reflect the idea that we need to invest effort in figuring things out. In the time of Avraham, this would have been easier to do, and hence Noach would not have built himself as much.

In the same vein, Rav Eliyahu Eliezer Dessler, *zt"l*, states[40] that the greatest people became who they are because of their resistance to their environment.

> I taught one noble soul who traveled the world in search of the truth. He was both ingenious and wealthy. He went everywhere and, I'm sorry to say, tried almost everything. Then he discovered *Yiddishkeit*. "Reb Noach," he told me, "we have no competition." Today he is happily studying Torah in the Mir Yeshivah in Jerusalem and is raising a beautiful Jewish family.

These two facets of Noach's greatness — seeking truth and strengthening himself in the face of a wildly decadent civilization — bring us to the next two mind-sets.

The third mind-set: Beware of compromise

There is no question that we do not seek exposure to a bad environment. But if we must be exposed to it, we can — like Noach — become very great from it. Beware, though: the *Madreigas HaAdam* points out, and this is particularly true today, that in such times a person cannot compromise. There is no in between. The world out there is full of evil — very evil

---

40. *Michtav MeEliyahu*, vol. 1, pp. 157–60.

— influences, and there is no protection for the untrained or unprepared, especially among our youth.

The *Madreigas HaAdam* gives a beautiful parable:

> In times of peace, when a person travels first class, it is a sign of wealth. But during wartime, all the regular seats are filled with soldiers, and if a civilian wants to travel he must buy a first-class ticket regardless of his financial status. Noach had to travel first class in order to survive. Had he lived in Avraham's time, he would not have had to travel first class in order to get on the train that would lead him to discover the truth.

It is wartime. If we are forced, for whatever reason, to be surrounded by an impure environment, we must travel first class — without compromise. Various communities have different ways of dealing with the secular media, which has so much potential to harm us. But there can be no compromise, especially for our children, when it comes to exposure to the depravity that passes for entertainment today. It must be totally, unequivocally removed from our lives. This must be done with wisdom and circumspection, but it must happen if we wish to raise a healthy, happy generation of people who pursue and cherish Torah values and the joy that this brings.

The fourth mind–set: Seek truth through giving

The other opinion, that Noach's greatness was rooted in his search for truth, is also vital to remember, since it is part and parcel of what we do every day: we learn Torah and seek to understand the will of Hashem. There is also no question that if we truly seek the truth, we will become greater, even among a wicked generation.

Noach's search for truth was inextricably bound with his trait of loving-kindness. We can see the depth of his *chesed* by looking at how severely he was punished simply for being late with a feeding for one of the lions.[41] Hashem only holds a person up to a standard that he can meet; a harsh punishment for what seems to be a small infraction indicates that much is expected of him. If Noach was punished for a lapse in *chesed*, this means that Hashem knew he had a great capacity for kindness.[42]

What's the connection between seeking truth and doing *chesed*? Only someone who can get outside of himself, out of his egocentric view of life, can see the truth. And it is only by giving, by *chesed*, that we can escape our own egos.[43] We see this link between truth and *chesed* in many places in *Tanach*. Just a few examples:

The Gemara says[44] that the prophet Ovadiah lived at the same time as two wicked people (Achav and Izevel) and didn't learn from their evil. He will come and serve as a rebuke to Esav, who lived with his two righteous parents and did not learn from their goodness. Rivkah Imeinu lived with the wicked Lavan and Besuel and yet remained untouched by their influence. Yosef HaTzaddik, too, raised amazing children in a horrible environment.

Is there a common thread in all of this? Yes! The common thread is that all these personalities who remained uninfluenced by a negative environment were givers. Ovadiah fed 100 prophets. Rivkah, who fed Eliezer's camels, is the paradigm of

---

41. *Rashi* on *Bereishis* 7:23 relates that Noach was once late with the lion's meal and the beast attacked him.

42. The Beis HaLevi (beginning of *Miketz*) uses the same idea to explain why Yosef was punished so severely, with another two years in an Egyptian prison, just for asking the wine steward to intercede on his behalf. He must have been on a very high level of *bitachon* to merit such a severe punishment for doing what seems to us to be ordinary *hishtadlus*.

43. For more on this idea, see Mind-Set 32, "The Road to Self-Discovery: *Chesed*."

44. *Sanhedrin* 39b.

chesed, and Yosef fed the entire world. Esav, on the other hand, was a conqueror, one who took rather than gave.

Why should being a giver offer protection from bad surroundings? The authentic giver — as a confirmed seeker of truth — is unconcerned with how others view him and is therefore less likely to need to seek approval from his environment.

We learn from all these examples that we must seek the truth by going out of ourselves. We must go out of ourselves in order to become givers. And *we must become givers in order to protect ourselves from negative influences.*

> Rav Avraham Mordechai Brotstein, *zt"l*, the former secretary of the Eidah HaChareidis of Jerusalem, offered an interesting parallel of this paradigm to the laws of salting meat. As long as the meat, covered by salt, is "busy" giving out its blood, it will not reabsorb it. When you are busy giving to others, you don't absorb from the outside; you are too busy giving to be affected by what is going on around you.

Turning Ideas into Action

▶ *Arm yourself with good thoughts.*

When forced to interact with a negative, immoral environment, seek to reflect on the happiness to be found in a spiritual lifestyle. I tell people who have to travel on public transportation that although it is best to focus on Torah and other healthy thoughts, sometimes this is hard to do. In that case, they should look around at the faces of old people. People who have lived a spiritual life, following spiritual ideals, are worth more the older they get and they are happier. Their advice is sought, and they treasure the time they have.

On the other hand, when a person lives a life centered on physicality, the older they get the sadder they get. Their bodies can no longer do the things that made them happy; they are limited in what they can eat and their vision deteriorates, depriving them of viewing the things that occupied their minds when they were younger. After a lifetime of focusing solely on transient things, their understanding of life is poor, and they suffer the infirmities of old age without the wisdom they need to cope with those infirmities. As Rav Avigdor Miller, *zt"l*, put it, "Old age does not give wisdom when you spent your days in the Pitkin Avenue Theater" (the movie theater near Yeshivas Rabbeinu Chaim Berlin when it was located in Brownsville).

Therefore, when you see an elderly sage, focus on the honor he gets and the fact that people are constantly seeking his advice. The meaning and purpose he has in his old age is a result of a well-lived life. Rav Miller, *zt"l*, once saw an elderly man in an old-age home studying assiduously. Rav Miller commented that the person was happily preparing for the big exam he would be taking after 120 years. Indeed, the Talmud[45] calls the citizens of the Babylonian city Massa Machsaya "hard of heart" because they saw the great biannual honor that the sages of the Torah were accorded, and this did not move any of them to convert to Judaism. Let us be the ones to look and see and learn from what we observe.

▶ *Do a chesed.*

Try to find an opportunity to do *chesed* each day. When people are involved in caring for others, their minds do not focus on the selfishness that permeates this pleasure-seeking society, and it can't influence them as deeply. These kindnesses need not be large; a smile directed at someone we meet is important and valuable.

---

45. *Berachos* 17b.

Life at a Crossroads: The Mystery of Time

There is no time like the present and we exist only in the present, right? The past is gone; the future is yet to be. Yet the present is the crossroads between the future and our past, and we ignore the future and the past at our peril.

Chanukah: A lesson on treasuring time

There is a famous dispute between Beis Hillel and Beis Shammai regarding the Chanukah lights. Beis Hillel holds that we should mark the number of days that have passed by lighting one light on the first night, two the second, and so on (the ruling that we actually follow today). Beis Shammai says that we should focus on the days that are yet to come: light eight lights on the first night, seven on the second, and so on. Rav

Moshe Schwab, *zt"l*, says[46] that the dispute refers to two different perspectives on the passage of time.

A person is always standing at a crossroads; his present is the point where his past and his future intersect. This means that at any given moment, he should not focus only on the present; he must live in the present, look toward the future, and bear his past in mind. By looking at the number of days that lie ahead of us, Beis Shammai teaches that a person must look to what is coming up. Beis Hillel says that we have to look back and see what we have already accomplished, and thus our lighting on Chanukah reflects the days that have passed.

One thing is clear: *we need to see time as a totality, realize that our present is connected to both our past and our future.*

There is no question that both attitudes have merit. The disagreement was merely a question of which one is dominant.

Present vs. future, specific vs. big picture

A mature person, the person who is governed by his intellect, can see the big picture and puts things in their perspective. No one thing, not even the present, can overwhelm him, because there is a larger picture. When a person is governed by emotions, though, he sees only the immediate, and he can't see past the specific: the present.

The ability to focus on the future allows us to respond to events more effectively. If we are able to bear the future in mind, we may choose to keep silent now and wait for the right moment to say what must be said. We can decide to look away from certain negative behaviors, knowing that this may be the best way to deal with them.

With children, for example, it's often appropriate to look away from specific, current misbehavior in anticipation of improvement in the future by letting them experience the natural

---

46. *Ma'archei Lev*, vol. 2, p. 76.

consequences of their present actions. For instance, if children leave their clothing in a mess on the floor, rather than battling over it now, as our emotions would urge us to do, it's more effective to look away and simply let the mess grow worse — until the children see that they have no clean clothing or become disgusted with the way their room looks. Of course, you need to tell your children, calmly and lovingly, that this is what you are planning to do. Otherwise, they may mistake your inaction as a sign that you also don't place great significance on cleanliness and order.

By realizing that there is more to life than the present — that terribly messy room that is bothering you so much — and that the future will be "cleaner" if you don't make a fight, you will allow the children to learn that cleanliness is important. Ultimately they will become considerate enough to put their clothing in the hamper.

Time: Treasure it!

Why is the day of death called "*tov me'od*," very good?[47] Because knowing that our time is limited in this world causes us to treasure our time. We know that we have to count our days, and this makes us use them more meaningfully, and therefore more happily.

> Every summer, Rav Yosef Chaim Sonnenfeld, *zt"l*, would go to the Diskin orphanage in the city's outskirts, for the benefit of the healthier air. In the summer of 1931, Rav Yosef Chaim cut his vacation short. When asked why, he explained that he felt that he was nearing his end, and he didn't want people to have to carry him the greater distance to the Mount of Olives. When asked how he could have such morbid thoughts, he

---

47. *Bereishis Rabbah*, ch. 9; see also *Gesher HaChaim*, pt. 3, Ch. 2.

said that from the time that he had reached middle age, the thought of his last day never left him, but it caused him no ill effects, no depression or anxiety. He truly understood that the day of death is "very good."[48]

A person can appreciate the day of death if he doesn't live only in the present. The day of death is *"tov me'od,"* very good, when it is part of a context: life in the Next World.

> The Vilna Gaon's sister once came to visit him. They had not seen each other for many, many years. Fifteen minutes into the visit, he said that he needed to resume learning. She began to cry, saying that all he had for her after so many years was 15 minutes. He pointed to the one white hair on his mustache and said, "This is my first summons from the heavenly court. I must heed it."

If a person lives only for the moment, then fear of death can make him hedonistic or selfish: "eat, drink, and be merry, for tomorrow we die." But when it is in the context of the future, a future of *Olam Haba*, it lends meaning and joy to life in this world.

Appreciating time and the difference between Esav and Aharon

I once heard the late *mashgiach* of the Kamenitz Yeshiva in Jerusalem, Rav Moshe Aharon Stern, *zt"l*, point out that the difference between Esav and Aharon was in the way they related to time.

Aharon felt deeply disappointed when he was not included in the dedication of the Mishkan, a one-time event. Esav, on the other hand, was willing to sell his birthright: the privilege

---

48. See *Guardian of Jerusalem* (Arscroll / Mesorah, 1983), p. 471.

of serving in the Sanctuary, which at that point still belonged to the firstborn. He was ready to give it up because he knew that a few hundred years later, with the *cheit ha'eigel*, the firstborn would lose the privilege. He felt it wasn't worth the trouble and decided he didn't want it.

Esav, with his superficial, live-in-the-present vision, did not value each and every moment, not only for itself, but as part of an eternal picture. He never saw the larger context, didn't realize that the opportunity presented to him as the firstborn was part of something eternal.

Aharon, on the other hand, truly appreciated the value of each and every moment. He realized that every minute of time is part of something vast, and so being deprived of something unique that lasted only a short time could still be bitterly disappointing.

We can either despise time because each moment is so small, or we can treasure it, by connecting it to the big picture. For Esav, time was just a collection of separate moments, each short-lived and ultimately unimportant. For Aharon HaKohen, every minute was part of a past and a future and thus something to be treasured.

> How important is a small amount of time? The story is told of a chassidic Rebbe who smoked a pipe. He once watched someone empty his pipe, clean it, refill it with tobacco, and relight it. In that time the Rebbe was able to complete the study of a page of Talmud. He never smoked a pipe again. The price was too high.

Turning Ideas into Action ▶

▶ *Learn a topic of Torah a little at a time.*

The Rosh Yeshivah, *zt"l*, taught us to value even small bits of time. One way to learn this is by taking a specific activity that takes minimal time and seeing, through doing this activity consistently, how much can be accomplished. For example, pick a Torah topic. Take 10 minutes or less each day and learn a small portion of this part of Torah. The topic should have the following attributes:

1. The progress should be clearly measurable, such as a paragraph of *Kitzur Shulchan Aruch* or a chapter in *Navi* or Mishnah.

2. It should not be too difficult; study a work in English if that's easier for you.

3. It should be something that interests you.

4. Invest thought not only in what to learn, but when and where: the time chosen should not be too risky, such as right before you leave the house in the morning, and the place should be a relatively quiet one.

5. Be consistent: stick to the same time and place whenever you study this particular topic. Measure how much you have learned in a month's time and you will be amazed at the degree of accomplishment. In addition, I recommend that you should not consider how much ground was covered as much as how well the material is retained. That is:

6. During these 10 minutes a day, devote time to review the previous days' learning. You can also take a few days every other week and devote them solely to review. At the end of a month, you can derive pleasure from the clarity with which you know what you have learned, even if it is only 10 or so chapters of *Navi* or half a *masechta* of *Mishnayos*. This may also spur you to adopt cumulative review for all your Torah learning. By doing so, even those who cannot devote large amounts of time are well on their way to loving Torah and becoming true Torah scholars.

▶ *Build your appreciation muscles.*

Another fantastic use of a small amount of time is to take five minutes, twice a day, to reflect about someone you know and notice some good trait that he or she has. Write it down and
    1. appreciate knowing the person,
    2. savor that trait — enjoy it — and then
    3. think about how that trait can find expression in your own life.

It's better to remain focused on one particular individual for as long as your thinking is still fresh. It would be great if that person were your spouse. And if you can keep it up for life, that would be amazing!

The reason that this exercise is divided into several actions is because many of us can't think creatively for more than a few minutes. When you have a text to follow, as in exercise 1, it anchors you, and you can utilize 10 minutes at one go, but when you have no "tracks" to follow or a less clearly defined task, you tend to lose your train of thought after a few minutes.[49] Of course,

---

49. I am not recommending you try to hold any one thought in your mind for five minutes. This is extremely difficult to do. To help us improve our con-

with this exercise it is even more important to find a quiet place where you will not be distracted or disturbed.

One important note: There is no intention here to make you utilize every single five minutes of every single day. This is too difficult for most of us to do and will frustrate us or, worse, cause us to fixate too much on every passing moment. The Rosh Yeshivah, *zt"l*, did indeed do this each and every day, but he was a very happy and relaxed person, since he had worked toward this for many decades.

---

centration, Rav Avigdor Miller, *zt"l*, once gave us an assignment to think about one thing and one thing only for as long as we could. It could be a *pasuk* or a statement from Chazal; the main idea was to learn to hold one idea in our minds and think about it for as long as we could. This was done in order to develop our ability to concentrate. He said that it was extremely difficult to hold a thought for five minutes; he had done it in Slabodka as a *talmid* there, and it was a watershed moment in his life.

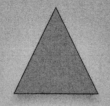

CHAPTER 5

Finding Our Inner World

People and Animals: What Makes Us Human

D ogs leap with joy when they hear their owner arriving home and get excited over a nice juicy hamburger. Cats purr with contentment when stroked, and a mother bear has com-passion for her cub. Animals have feelings, like humans do. Is there a difference? What makes our emotions uniquely human?

Animals feel, people feel — what's the difference?

While an animal can feel anger, fear, or joy, it can't think about its feelings. *Man, however, is capable of thinking about his thoughts and feelings.* This is the crux of what it means to be human: to be able, and therefore *obligated*, to evaluate one's situation before choosing, with one's free will, how to react to the situation.

Awareness vs. instinct

If we examine this idea further, we will find several vital differences between the emotions of man and the emotions of animals:

1. *An animal reacts to its surroundings.* When confronted with a predator, for instance, it doesn't choose to be afraid; its fearful response is instinctive. *A human being, on the other hand, is expected to choose.* He chooses not only how to react to the immediate situation, but he also chooses how to affect the situation, both now and with an eye to the future. He must therefore understand the situation, not merely be in it. We see this in the many awe-inspiring stories of men and women in concentration camps who overcame the instinctive fear of death to keep mitzvos or help others.

> The Bluzhever Rebbe, *zt"l*, was reciting the *shehecheyanu* blessing as he lit the Chanukah menorah in Bergen-Belsen when a Bundist, a member of the socialist secular Bund political party in Poland, came up to him and asked how the Rebbe could possibly feel joy in such a place. The Bluzhever responded that he, too, once had the same question. Then he saw how many Jews, at the risk of their lives, came to partake of the menorah lighting, and he was uplifted at the merit of such true joy. "Just as these Jews will never give up," he said, "one day we will rebuild." Years later, on a visit to Poland, Reb Nechemia Frankel met this Bundist, who told him to "tell Rabbi Spira that he saved my life. He will understand."

> Another story that I heard when I was a guest in the home of Rav Pinchas Goldschmidt, *shlita*, the chief rabbi of Moscow and perhaps the leading rabbinic figure in Europe, took place in Auschwitz.

The *rosh hakahal* (community leader) of a certain Eastern European community who was an old-time Communist mentioned to Rav Goldschmidt that he fasted on Yom Kippur even though he had no connection to religion. Why? In Auschwitz there was a deal between those who fasted on Yom Kippur and those who didn't. The fasters would give their Yom Kippur portion to those who weren't fasting. In exchange, they would receive half of the non-fasters' portion the next day.

One of the fasters came to the *rosh hakahal* before Yom Kippur and offered him his portion, but in the exchange he did not want the half portion of the *rosh hakahal's* ration the next day. Instead he wanted the promise that if the *rosh hakahal* got out of the camp alive, he would keep Yom Kippur for the rest of his life. The *rosh hakahal* survived and searched for years to find this person whose dedication to Hashem and His Torah transcended the deep and bitter hunger of Auschwitz.[1]

2. *An animal has no awareness that one day it will die.* This is because there is no reason for it to have such an awareness. An animal has no existence beyond this one and hence does not have to prepare for anything. It would be an unnecessary cruelty if the animal were aware of its mortality. *A human being, on the other hand, must know that his existence in this world is finite.* Such knowledge is a kindness, since it would be the ultimate cruelty to deprive him of the opportunity to prepare for a different, eternal existence. The awareness of his mortality in this world, coupled with the awareness of his eternal destiny, has a vital and overwhelming influence on how man uses his emotions: will they control him, or will he

---

1. Years later I saw this story in *Yated Ne'eman* (*Shelach* 5773). The *rosh hakahal* was named, and the story recorded that his fellow Jew had identified himself as "Farkash from Munkacz."

choose to shape them in a manner that will earn him eternal happiness?[2]

3. *A human being can exist in a world different from his present physical place.* For instance, a person in a very difficult situation can choose to put his mind elsewhere and not allow his present circumstance to destroy his equilibrium. This reaction is a defense mechanism that helps numb the person to an otherwise intolerable situation. (Of course, taken too far, this can be a form of denial or even mental illness.)

Mori V'Rabi, *zt"l*, would weep when he read the *pasuk*, "I will remove from you your heart of stone and give to you a heart of flesh."[3] He interpreted the "heart of stone" as the symbol of the suffering of the Jewish people in the days before Mashiach. The situation would be so bad that no one with a true awareness could bear it, so Hashem would give us hearts of stone. He would numb us so that we could withstand the sorrows and tragedies of the era immediately preceding the redemption.

Mind control

The ability to view our affairs effectively, and not allow situations to overwhelm us, gives us another advantage over animals. People who are able to control their minds are capable of resisting others' attempts to control their essence. They are using that which is uniquely human: the ability to think about and decide how they will view a certain situation.[4]

Often we're unable to control our emotions once a situation is upon us, especially when we are taken by surprise. If we can learn how to project, in advance, possible unpleasant, distressing, or even dangerous situations, we can decide what our thoughts, attitudes, and reactions will be when we are con-

---

2. See *Gesher HaChaim*, pt. 3, Ch. 4.
3. *Yechezkel* 36:26.
4. See Maharal, *Derech Chaim*, on *Avos* 6:2, s.v. *"v'ha'inyan."*

fronted by them (of course, don't let your imagination run wild with "what ifs"). These "simulations" should be repeated and reviewed in our minds many times. Then, when the situation we've visualized does arise, we will more likely be able to control our reactions and respond with the best possible choices, using our best judgment.

What we are really doing is seeing the future and pulling it into our present. We call this process "training," and you don't have to be a professional EMT or an air force pilot to do it. We all need to "train" ourselves to use our best judgment in stressful life situations. This is a powerful use of free will: to not just react to a present situation, but to "see" the future and internalize the proper response.

In time, these reactions will become natural for us, and we can continue to grow in learning to project and perform maturely and calmly in even the most challenging life situations.

Turning Ideas into Action

▶ *Start training: prepare yourself for challenges.*

Take the time to think about difficult situations that arise in your life, and consider what the best responses should be. Think about one situation at a time, and review whatever behavior and responses you think would be best, until they become second nature.

▶ *Compile a list.*

In the same vein, compile a list of responses that are beneficial in most situations, and, again, review them frequently. Preparation will help you respond, naturally and automatically, to situations where you are unsure of what to do. Well-thought-out mental attitudes and measured responses are usually right and help weather difficult and unfamiliar challenges. This list can include:

1. Whatever a person says to me, I will remain silent or respond softly and briefly.

2. I will never accuse or confront someone, especially when I feel emotionally upset.

3. I will seek to notice what's right in a person or in a situation and nurture myself with it.

▶ *Back up your choices.*

Find a statement of Chazal or selection from a *sefer* that expresses any of the ideas that you have compiled, and review it many, many times until these ideas seep into your innermost self. One of my favorites is a line from the *Sefer HaYashar*, a classic work of Jewish thought that is attributed to the famous medieval Tosafist Rabbeinu Tam. It goes like this: "Anyone who restrains himself from anger will never regret it."[5] *Anyone* and *never* are powerful words coming from someone who is famous for being concise and accurate in whatever he wrote.

---

5. See *Sefer HaYashar, Shaar Hashishi*, s.v., *Ve'ha'middah ha'sheinis.*

Dancing to the Music: Harnessing the Emotions

*A*t times emotions overpower us, causing us to do things we know are not right. Sometimes our emotional outbursts cause pain to others or even to ourselves. Yet humans are emotional beings, and our emotions are an integral part of us. It is our emotions that advertising and public relations campaigns manipulate in order to make us think and act the way they want. Let us explore the proper role of emotions in our personality and learn how to dance to our own music.

Building a high-functioning emotion

The heart is the center of the emotions, and it is constantly pulsating, moving, pumping. A working heart — and working emotions — are an important sign of life. This is healthy as long as the emotions are controlled by the steady and stable intellect.

Emotion is a vital part of being human, but it is not meant to control us. Emotions can't see the future. They tend to react to the immediate situation. The wisdom of the intellect, on the other hand, foresees the outcome of an emotional outburst. The intellect reins in the emotions to allow for a patient and reasonable reaction. Healthy people have both their intellect and emotions working in tandem.

The *madreigah*, the level, of a person in this world is a function of his ability to control and channel his emotions. This world is the "*olam hama'aseh*," the world of action, and it is the emotions that spur us to act.[6] But a strong emotional response does not necessarily imply a mature emotion. A balanced and mature emotion is created by a person's ability to *control* the emotion, and this is what establishes his level of righteousness in his behavior and actions.

In order to establish an ability to control emotions — to master our most powerful source of energy — we have to develop a strong and stable inner reality.

Our internal reality

Stability comes from an internal orientation, since the outside world keeps changing. The only thing constant that we have is our internal reality. This stable reality is intellectual, not emotional, and has two possible sources: our internal, moral conscience or Torah study.

A strong internal reality gives us the strength to resist the temptation to compromise our Torah beliefs and values in order to gain recognition, power, and prestige from the secular, hedonistic society we live in. In fact, this is the source of the strength that we draw upon so that our *Yiddishkeit* will flourish in an alien culture.

---

6. See Rav Tzadok HaKohen, *Tzidkas HaTzaddik* 248.

Madison Avenue, the heart of the advertising industry, constantly bombards us with advertisements that suggest that we are missing out on life if we don't sample all the pleasures the world has to offer: "You mean you didn't get that car or go on that vacation? You're missing out! You need it! You deserve it!"

Rav Shmuel Berenbaum, *zt"l*, the rosh yeshivah of the Mirrer Yeshiva in Brooklyn, once blessed us that we should love Torah as much as the big corporations love money, and yet they give away so much of their beloved money to pay for advertising. If they weren't sure that the advertisements would earn more money than they cost, they surely wouldn't invest in them. They are confident that the message they are selling will find its targets. But the belief, constantly reinforced by advertising, that we are missing something in our lives is a powerful and pervasive source of unhappiness. Only when our happiness has an internal-oriented anchor can we say no to these advertisements. When we allow ourselves to be led by our internal conscience, and not external compulsions, then we can say, "No, it's not true that sampling all the pleasures of the world will make me happy."

> A radio talk show host once called me, live, to tell me that I had won a free weekend in Spain. He was stunned when I said that I wasn't interested. A person who has an internal compass of where happiness lies has no need for external "imports" of materialism and diversions to make him happy. Though I can't claim to have perfected my inner world, I did know enough to realize that a Spanish weekend was not the way to happiness.

As an aside, the study of economics is predicated on the assumption that there is an unlimited amount of wants but a limited amount of resources. Though the second half of the premise — that resources are limited — is true in this finite world, the first part is not true. *There should not be an unlimited amount of wants in a person's life.* When I have what I need, and I have the resources to pay for it, I have no need to economize; I am wealthy. A person I know manages money for wealthy people who spend more than they earn. When I purchase what I need with only the resources that Hashem has given me, I have more money than they do!

This is just one way that our internal reality, and not our external environment, should drive how we live our life.

> Wanting to confirm my kosher meal, I once spent close to 15 minutes listening to an airline recording telling me how important my call was to them. I finally gave up. At boarding, the stewardess greeted me with the news that since my kosher meal had not been confirmed, it was not available. I wasn't upset; I had brought food with me in case there was no meal. This is a paradigm for life: the less I am dependent on what goes on outside me, the more stable I will be.

A tzaddik's emotions

The *tzaddik* is in control of his emotions and gives them free rein only when the intellect says to do so. We might see great men being either stoic or emotional, even to an extreme, but it is all a purposeful response.

> Mori V'Rabi, *zt"l*, was able to withstand great pain. A *talmid* of his once accompanied him to a medical examination. Before beginning the procedure, the doctor needed to evaluate how much pain Mori V'Rabi could withstand. On a scale of pain tolerance, where 10 was the most painful, he reached nine before he said that the pain had become intolerable. The *talmid* asked that the test be done on him, and he was only able to withstand a two. On the other hand, I had the privilege of accompanying Mori V'Rabi on his first visit to the Kosel

HaMa'aravi. We were walking down Armenian Patriarch Road when the Wall came into view. Immediately he broke down into intense sobbing.

Similarly, Rav Yisroel Ginsberg, *shlita*, of the Yeshiva of Staten Island is quoted as saying that when Rav Shach, *zt"l*, needed an operation on his leg, the doctor warned him that the general anesthetic he would receive would affect his ability to learn with a clear head for several days. On hearing that, Rav Shach refused the anesthetic, even though the doctor told him that without it the operation would be so painful that he would have to be tied down during the procedure. Rav Yisroel was one of those present at the operation, and he testified that Rav Shach did not utter a groan. This same Rav Shach broke down sobbing upon hearing of the deaths of three Israeli soldiers with whom he shared no direct connection of any sort.

The *rasha*, the wicked man, is given over completely to his heart, to his emotional reality; he sees only the immediate and does not consider the long term. Not only is he driven by his passions, but he is more likely to become depressed because he doesn't see the big picture, that what is happening is part of G-d's plan, which is always good.

We carry around our own music, or else we dance to someone else's. *Happiness is defined as the ability to carry our music around with us.* And what is the rhythm, the music, that defines us? The stability that comes from the understanding that all that we go through is from G-d and that we have a place in His big picture. Since the *tzaddik* is able to see the bigger picture, no given occurrence can cause him to lose control over his emotions.

In order to cope with adversity, and not give ourselves over to despondency and hopelessness, we, too, need to train ourselves to see the big picture. *We must be conscious of the reality that whatever happens is an expression of Hashem's will.* When we can do this, then we can have control over our feelings and make our own music rather than dancing to the music of others.

As a beautiful example of this, Rav Mattisyahu Salomon, *shlita*, the *mashgiach* in Lakewood's Beth Medrash Govoha, says that Hashem expects the Jewish heart to feel genuine pain for a bereaved family while paying a *shivah* call and then to be able to cross the street to a *sheva berachos* celebration and feel true joy for the newly married bride and groom. This is also true in the years when Tishah B'Av, the day when we mourn the destruction of our Temple in Jerusalem, falls on Sunday. As long as it's Shabbos we rejoice with the Shabbos Queen, and as soon as it ends we are able to sit on the floor in deep mourning.

The optimist and the ba'al bitachon

When we make our own music, we must be able to temper it and filter it through our intellect. This is the vital difference between the optimist, someone who expects things to turn out well, and the *ba'al bitachon*, the person who has complete trust in Hashem that everything is good no matter what happens.

An optimist is someone who expects things to work out, and that is generally a healthy attitude. But we must draw an important line when these expectations turn into a *need* or a given. That's when disappointment can become overwhelming.

Frum people visiting the Kosel for the first time are sometimes disappointed. They expect a huge spiritual rush, and when it doesn't happen they feel let down. On the other hand, people who weren't expecting anything often come away with real, soul-stirring inspiration.[7] A *true* optimist, better known

---

7. Usually surprise is the enemy of intellect, since we are unable to access our intellect as quickly as our emotions; when surprised, we act on our emotions and often we're sorry. In this case, though, surprise is the *friend* of emotion, because it allows a person to experience the inspiration and *kedushah* of a place like the Kosel HaMa'aravi without misguided optimism.

as a "*ba'al bitachon*," is someone who truly trusts Hashem and lives in a happy world knowing that he has a powerful Friend taking care of him. This kind of optimist does not expect, as a given, that things will turn out exactly according to his specifications of what is "good."[8]

Often things that throw a person into emotional turmoil turn out to be not a misfortune at all; to the contrary, they were very good, even if they didn't seem so at the time. When we know this intellectually, we can truly look forward to the future with optimism, for even what seems to be a misfortune will, we know, turn out to be very good.

Today's world can be perceived as being an unhappy one, but that's only if we walk to the drumbeats of other people. When we are able to internalize the music of Hashem's drum, the only true music in the world, then everything has its place: we give free vent to our emotions when appropriate and withhold them when it is correct, making our lives a beautiful blend of balance and color.

---

8. See Chazon Ish, *Emunah U'Bitachon*, beginning of Ch. 2, for a thorough treatment of this idea.

▶ *Take a lesson from watching the way others handle their emotions.*

Observe how people's emotions affect their lives. This can be for good, such as when a person genuinely empathizes with someone else's distress or joy, or it can be negative, such as when anger is expressed too powerfully. Do this exercise without judging the person; you never know how another person was raised or what other circumstances brought him to this situation. Rather, the point is to internalize, through quiet thought and introspection, the richness of a life, in this world and the Next, of those who have warm and positive emotions. It is best to focus on one person, until that particular lesson becomes deeply embedded in you.

▶ *Treasure a particular positive emotion.*

It can be a feeling of gratitude or satisfaction at achieving a certain goal or any happy moment. These moments often come without your expecting them, and they can be fleeting if you don't take the time and effort to internalize them. Keep a notebook where you record these moments, or a computer file if that works better for you. Or, as we have already mentioned in this book, "freeze the moment" for you to retrieve at will. When the moment occurs, memorize your surroundings: is it light or dark, warm or cold? Take an inventory of the details. This allows you to access the emotion in the future, because it is part of a complete experience.

No Surprises: The Mitzvos of the Heart

*F*eelings spring forth from the heart; they are genuine and intense. Yet the "mitzvos of the heart" command us to feel certain things. Can feelings and intense emotion be controlled? Can you command someone to have an emotion, as indeed the Torah does in the most basic areas of life, such as fearing Hashem, loving Him, not coveting others' possessions, and rejoicing on Yom Tov?[9]

There is no question that a person can control his feelings, or else the Torah would not have commandments that bring our emotions into play. There are also rabbinical commandments that tell us to feel certain emotions, such as mourning on Tishah B'Av. But how can we control how we feel at any given time?

---

9. The Ibn Ezra on *Shemos* 20:14 asks how it is that the Torah can command us not to covet. We can ask the same question about any of the positive emotions that the Torah commands us to have.

Two enemies: surprise and laziness

Rav Tzadok HaKohen says[10] that the chief tools of the *yetzer hara* are surprise and laziness. It seems to me that surprise is what makes it hard to control our emotions, while laziness defeats the intellect.

When we're taken by surprise, when we find ourselves unprepared, our emotions can take control of us, instead of our controlling them. Laziness, on the other hand, is the enemy of the *seichel*: we don't use our minds, and we become too lazy to think things through.

The solution to problems of *seichel* is increased intellectual effort, and *the solution to emotional problems is to decrease the levels of surprise.* We must not let our emotions sneak up on us. The more we can understand why we feel something, the more we will be able to control our emotional response.

Emotions know only the present. Introducing the intellect connects the present to the past and the future; we take the time to see the big picture — the consequences of our actions — and inject a calming influence on our uncontrolled feelings.

Controlling emotions through thought and action

The commandments connected to our emotions are really commands to do something that will help bring about that emotion. We can do this in two ways:

1. *Through thought* — developing an attitude that will bring about a specific emotion through using our thought processes.

2. *Through action* — doing things that will bring about the emotion.

---

10. *Resisei Lailah* 38.

Control through thought

How can we use our thoughts to develop attitudes that will then control our emotional responses?

By thinking things through, we can react not with unbridled emotion, but with emotion controlled by careful consideration. One of the most important principles to remember about effective thinking is that *real thinking can only take place in an atmosphere of quiet*. Quiet time lets us muse about all aspects of a situation so we are not taken by surprise, which, as we said, is the great enemy of the emotion. Quiet time allows us to look at things differently and therefore react to them differently.

> I heard from Rav Avigdor Miller, *zt"l*, that a husband should pause a few moments outside his door before entering the house at suppertime to think about what is going on there. The idea is to prepare himself for what might really be going on, so that seeing the children fighting, or the kitchen a mess, or dinner not ready, won't provoke an angry outburst. A little quiet — a little thought — allows for control of the emotions so that the response is correct.

Focused thought can also evoke vital emotions, such as gratitude:

> Rav Miller would also urge people to think of some way to bring joy to their wives. He advised husbands to think of different ways of complimenting their spouse. One of the byproducts of this is to help the husband focus on the fact that his wife is, indeed, a wonderful, special person. This keeps him from taking her for granted and increases his positive feelings for his wife.

Control through action

The active mitzvos, such as keeping Shabbos, davening, or Torah study, are meant to touch our emotions through deeds and experiences. The emotion knows only the present; it is experiential. Therefore it is affected by action. So we are given a clear, obvious act to do that brings about a change in a person. *When the Torah is commanding us with regard to our emotions, it is actually telling us to do something that will help us achieve the desired emotion.* The Rambam seems to use this approach.[11] When he discusses fear and love of Hashem, he asks, "What is the path to achieving love and fear of Him?" He then goes on to describe actions that lead to these emotions.

Mori V'Rabi, *zt"l*, suggests that the reason that the Torah commands us to eat meat and drink wine on the festivals is to foster the emotion of joy, which is a Torah commandment.[12] Women and children have other means by which they can feel joy on a *Yom Tov*, such as getting new clothing, shoes, or jewelry, and it is the responsibility of the husband or father to provide them. We are enjoined to do something that will foster the emotion.

When we wish to feel a positive emotion, such as love and fear of Hashem or joy during a festival, or conversely, when we want to avoid feeling an emotion, such as a paralyzing fear, we are going to be looking for something to do in order to achieve this.[13]

The Pesach Seder, says the *Shiurei Da'as*,[14] is a prime example of this type of influence. Through the actions we do on

---

11. See *Hilchos Yesodei HaTorah*, Ch. 2.

12. See *Devarim* 16:14–15.

13. See *Sefer HaChinuch*, mitzvah 488, where it is noted that every human being needs times of joy, in the same way that a person needs food, rest, and sleep. Although this idea is outside the purview of this book, it deserves to be mentioned, since it is a vital guideline for a successful life. But as with all of life's necessities, it's important that you control them, not that they control you. We choose the venue of these times of joy and the amount of time we will spend on them, and they do not choose for us.

14. Rav Yosef Yehudah Leib Bloch, *zt"l*, *Nishmas HaTorah*.

Seder night, we begin to experience the feeling of liberation of *Yetzias Mitzrayim* and awe and appreciation of the miracles. It is the sublime nature of these acts that give them such power. The message is subliminal, and therefore it enters our emotional reality without arousing the intellect's opposition.[15]

These actions have a deep effect on our emotional life, because *the things we do are concrete and leave their mark on a person.*

It is for this reason that after *Krias Yam Suf* the Jews began their Song of the Sea with the drowning of the horse and rider. Even though they had seen many great prophetic visions, the death of the Egyptians also affected them physically and so made a stronger impression on them.

But how do we avoid the negative emotions?

With regard to avoiding negative emotions, it is often a good idea to find a specific action to do (such as trying to bring a smile to someone's face or calling a friend to see how he is), but sometimes our response will not be something active. Instead, we search for a thought or attitude that we place in our minds to ward off the negative emotion.

So what can I do, using my mind and thought processes, to allow me to overcome negative, bitter thoughts and emotions, and perhaps even grow from them?

Can you find something right in a tough situation, and nourish yourself with that? Maybe you can uncover a virtue in a

---

15. It is the nature of the intellect to oppose. This is why, says the Maharal, Jews can be so argumentative (see *Shem MiShmuel*, beginning of *Vayeitzei*, which cites the Maharal). Although it's often important to control emotions with the intellect, if I want to circumvent the intellect in order to evoke certain emotions, I will try to receive the message subliminally. This is a common marketing ploy, such as posting advertisements everywhere telling you to "drink Coke." When I read the ad with my intellect, I might say no, but if I see it everywhere without really paying attention, eventually I will absorb the message. We can use "subliminal advertising" in a positive way by allowing experiences such as the Seder affect us.

person you are annoyed with or in a situation that you find less than pleasing.

Think about someone you perceive as being stubborn. You can focus on the fact that this person is, at the same time, kind and thoughtful. Even better, you can see how the trait of stubbornness also manifests itself as a tenacity that has brought about many positive results.

> The *Chovos HaLevavos* tells of the wise man who was walking with his students.[16] They passed the carcass of a dead animal. The students mentioned the terrible smell, and their teacher replied, "But its teeth are so white!"
>
> I know a wonderful Jew, paralyzed in an automobile accident, who has taken this new reality in his life to experience joy in a way that he never dreamed of before the crash.

The first thought: Beyond our responsibility

Several years ago, at a meeting in Eretz Yisrael of yeshivah *mashgichim*, Rav Mattisyahu Salomon, *shlita*, *mashgiach* of Beth Medrash Govoha in Lakewood, made a point that I believe to be nothing less than one of the fundamental underpinnings of mental health. He said that we are not held responsible for an improper thought that enters our mind; we are held culpable for holding on to it.[17] If we don't retain the thought, then we are not responsible for it entering our mind, because over that we had no control.

In other words, *we are not responsible for the thoughts that enter our minds; we are responsible for what we do with them when they have already entered our minds.*

---

16. *Sha'ar HaKeniyah*, Ch. 10.

17. See *Tzidkas HaTzaddik* 234, which says that it is for this reason that we aren't forbidden to have idle thoughts, since this is beyond our control.

It follows that when we have thoughts or emotions that we would rather not dwell on, we should not bemoan the fact that these thoughts or emotions entered our mind. Rather, we should find a means of effectively eliminating them since it is our responsibility to determine what thoughts or emotions we dwell on.

How do we do this?

Rav Michel Twerski, *shlita*, of Milwaukee once said to me that a person can be trapped into allowing improper thoughts to occupy his mind by constantly thinking about them, even if all he is doing is trying his best to ignore them. It's analogous, said Rav Michel, to when someone is knocking at my door, someone whom I don't want to let in. Even if I don't let him in, if I focus on his knock, he still has control over my consciousness, because it is his knocking that preoccupies me. Similarly, trying to ignore a thought, to push it out of my mind by force, is another way of actually holding on to the thought, even if indirectly.

If you don't want to let in the person who is knocking (or the thought!), it's much better to ignore the knock completely by keeping busy with thoughts that *you* wish to entertain. For example, the best way to stop thinking about green is to think about blue rather than constantly thinking about not thinking about green.

This is another example of our principle that *the best way to avoid something negative is to be involved in something positive.* Be involved in positive thoughts, and the negative ones will evaporate.

► Set aside some quiet time each day to think and exercise your intellect.

Preferably it should be in a quiet place, even though for many of us this is easier said than done. Take the time to think about when and where you can have this quiet time for contemplation. It can take place in your car, before you enter your home at the end of the day, or before you go to your place of work or study at the beginning of the day. The walk home from a train or bus can also be the set time for thinking.

► Walk around the block or down the street before entering your house.

Use this time to access the emotions that can enrich your life. You can decide which emotion to focus on; for example, gratitude for having a job or a proper place of study or for having a place to come home to. You can then attach that emotion to an action; for example, to the physical act of walking into your home or place of work or to the act of kissing the mezuzah upon entry.

► Take control of your thoughts.

When an unwanted thought enters your mind, there are several things you can do:

1. Calmly accept the fact that you are thinking this thought, but realize that you can think about other things as well. You are not chained to this particular thought.

2. A wise Jew told a student of mine who was plagued with unwanted thoughts to compile a collection of happy memories and replace an unwanted thought with one of his happy thoughts. I think that this can be extended to focusing on things that interest you, which can more easily compete with the uninvited thought.

3. Thinking a Torah thought can accomplish the same thing, and in addition it purifies the mind. Just as fire can *kasher* a metal vessel that became *tereifah* by removing any unwanted non-kosher food that was absorbed in the walls of the vessel through cooking, so Torah can purify a person's mind from something it should not have absorbed.[18]

4. Sometimes a person can't relieve himself of unwanted thoughts, and they can control his life and cause untold misery. In such cases, professional help can provide relief, and it should not be considered anything to be ashamed of.

▶ *Remember that Hashem loves you unconditionally.*

This is especially true when a person is suffering from something he or she can't control and wants to be free of. I recommend that people focus on the words that we say every day: "*Elokai neshamah shenasata bi tehorah hi* — Hashem, the soul that you placed within me is totally pure." Our souls are intrinsically and immutably pure; we are beloved to Hashem. This is especially true for those who observe Torah Judaism in today's hedonistic and materialistic world. Even those

---

18. See *Shem MiShmuel, Bereishis,* p. 96.

who know only that they are Jewish must know that there is no limit to Hashem's love for them, for their ancestors withstood so many bitter tests in order to be loyal to their Torah. Even Jews who are estranged from the Torah, yet refuse, against all odds and against all temptations, to intermarry deserve Hashem's love. We can't conceive of the love that Hashem has for all of us. May this knowledge carry us through these times of painful and seemingly insurmountable tests.

Knobs, Cups, and Flowers: Three Keys to Wisdom

T oday you can access the mega-mind of humanity with the click of a mouse or the tap of a finger. With just a little effort you can find facts, research history, locate obscure references, learn the temperature of anyplace on earth, and catch breaking news as it happens. But has all this information made us any wiser? Mori V'Rabi, zt"l, said, commenting on the technological revolution, "The buildings are getting bigger, and the people are getting smaller."

What transforms useless knowledge into meaningful wisdom? The answer can be found in the Menorah.

The symbol of Torah wisdom

The Menorah in the Temple, with its seven lights burning bright, symbolized Torah wisdom. It was decorated with three types of decorations: knobs, cups, and flowers.

These decorations hint to us how to acquire wisdom. How?

Rav Mordechai Dolinsky, *shlita*, says that the three decorations parallel the three abilities of the mind: the ability to retain information (the cups), the ability to think independently of outside stimulus (the knobs), and the ability to create new and beautiful ideas (the flowers).

I think that this beautiful idea can be taken further to reveal to us the way to acquire wisdom.

The cups and the first level of wisdom

The function of a cup — to hold that which is poured into it — parallels the mind's ability to retain information.

To become wise, we will *make sure to gather as much information as possible before making a decision on anything.* This first level of wisdom includes all the effort that we have to make in order to retain information that we have acquired. How do we ensure that we do so?

1. The information must be important to us.

2. We should review properly.

3. We should pray for *siyatta diShmaya* that our efforts will bear fruit.

4. We must develop the trait of humility. A humble person knows that there is much that he doesn't know. and he will make an effort to keep gathering as much information as he can.

Once we have gathered the necessary information, we must be able to mull it over. This brings us to the next level of wisdom.

The knobs and the second level of wisdom

Once we have achieved a high level of knowledge (that is, the "cup"), we need to be able to mull it over, to make it part of ourselves. A round disk, a complete circle, is the symbol of a mind that is whole and at peace. It parallels the mind's ability to "gather round," to withdraw into itself and disassociate from the outside environment in order to contemplate the knowledge it possesses.

For this we need two things:

1. a quiet environment and

2. an environment that will not distort wisdom through negative influences; that has no spiritual "static."

Finding the quiet from without, a quiet space without distractions, is actually the lower level of concentration. There is an even higher level: the ability to disassociate ourselves from the distractions that surround us, without necessarily needing a quiet environment, in order to achieve the concentration that enhances our ability to think productively and creatively.

When we become independent of our environment, then we have achieved the ability to concentrate in its highest, truest form. *"Concentration" is defined as the ability to carry around our quiet with us.* Stability derives from not being at the mercy of an ever-changing environment; for this, it is necessary to achieve peace of mind.

Peace of mind is the opposite of a soul that is scattered and unfocused; it is the opposite of being unable to concentrate, as it says, "There is no greater peace than peace of mind and no greater scatteredness than a scattered mind."[19] To attain this quiet, a person must be able to honestly focus and reflect on the inner truths of life, unaffected by what goes on around him.

There is no question that the ability to shut out the outside world is related to appreciating who we are and the Torah we learn. We can "live" inside ourselves without constantly needing to look outside ourselves for justification and encouragement.[20]

---

19. The Alter of Kelm, *Chochmah U'Mussar*, vol. 1, p. 282.

20. See Mind-Set 24, "Dancing to the Music: Harnessing Our Emotions," where this idea of an "internal reality" is discussed.

Rav Chaim Friedlander, *zt"l*, tells[21] of the time that Rav Yerucham Levovitz, *zt"l,* sent Rav Abba Grossbard with a question for the Chafetz Chaim when the Chafetz Chaim was already a very old man. Rav Grossbard found the Chafetz Chaim immersed in Torah study. He looked up, heard the question, thought about it, and gave an answer. He then asked if there was more, and when Rav Abba said there wasn't, the Chafetz Chaim immediately went back to his learning, as if there had been no interruption.

I had a similar experience when I entered the Steipler Gaon's small room. He looked up from the *sefer* he was learning, read the question put to him (he was deaf in his later years), and answered it. By the time I turned to leave, the Steipler was again fully immersed in his studies. Many others who visited the Steipler told the same tale.

In a similar story, my *chavrusa* once went to the Steipler's son, Rav Chaim Kanievsky, *shlita,* to discuss a difficult portion in *Bava Kamma.* When my *chavrusa* asked the question, he quoted the page number to Rav Chaim, who was in the middle of writing. Rav Chaim said nothing; he just handed him a Gemara *Bava Kamma* without looking up from his writing. My *chavrusa* opened it up and realized he had quoted the wrong page number; he was off by one page. Only when he told Rav Chaim the correct page number did Rav Chaim look up, ready to answer his question. And when he'd finished his response, Rav Chaim turned back to his writing, effortlessly picking up from where he'd left off. Rav Chaim's peace of mind was total, and therefore his concentration was total. Whatever he was doing, that was what

---

21. *Sifsei Chaim, Middas Avodas Hashem,* vol. 2, p. 58.

he was doing, with total dedication and attention, and no outside interruptions could distract him.

Great men have been asked a question in the middle of writing a sentence. They would stop, answer the question, and then continue writing the sentence as if there had been no interruption.

All of these stories display the incredible peace of mind these *gedolim* achieved. Whatever they did, they did with total focus; there was no tug-of-war inside them with different thoughts vying for their attention. Once their value system told them at each moment what they needed to do, at that moment their focus was total.

The flowers and the third level of wisdom

We are now ready, after achieving intellectual and emotional honesty, to create new and beautiful information. This is what the flowers of the Menorah represented: the ability to create new and beautiful ideas.

In addition we can now learn how to react to new, uncharted areas and questions in life. *We can listen deeply, and without bias, to others, because we are not dependent on being "right" in order to look good; we are deeply committed to the truth.* We will now have insights that have the stamp of truth. This is the area of wisdom that our *gedolei Yisrael* attained.

> Rav Zelig Pliskin, *shlita*, was deeply affected by a lecture given by Rav Mordechai Gifter, *zt"l*, his *rosh yeshivah* in Telshe Yeshivah in Wickliffe, Ohio. Rav Gifter had delivered the lecture to the entire yeshivah student body, and it was an intricate and beautiful piece of Talmudic wisdom. Suddenly, one of the students asked a question. Rav Mordechai stood there, thought for a moment, and then stated that he had been refuted and

stepped down. Rav Pliskin remarked that it would have been easy for the *rosh yeshivah* to brush aside the student's remarks, but he was more dedicated to the truth than to looking good.

The importance of the process

I believe these three powers of the mind follow the sequence in which they appear in the Torah: cups, knobs, and flowers. First, and especially during our youth when our minds are the most retentive, we need to be "cups" — to absorb as much knowledge as possible. Then we need to be able to mull over what we have learned in tranquillity and silence, as represented by the knobs. Finally, we can produce beautiful new ideas — "flowers" — with this information.[22]

With these three powers in place, we can view the world and the never-ending challenges that it brings to us in a fruitful and productive way. We must be willing to learn and absorb from those wiser than we, then develop our thinking powers, and then we will, eventually and with Hashem's help, be able to successfully navigate the somewhat turbulent seas of life — and help others do so as well.

---

22. See the Gra on *Mishlei* 6:8, where he discusses the same idea. He says that when a person is young, he should "gather his grain" — that is, learn a lot of Torah — since at this time his young mind's ability to retain information is great. Later, when his mind is more mature, he should "grind up the grain"; that is, reflect on the knowledge he has gained. He says that this is what is meant by the *mishnah* in the third chapter of *Avos* that "if there is no grain" (information, likened here to Torah), then "there is no flour" ("ground-up" Torah). If, in the end, when you're old, you don't grind up your Torah knowledge and think about it deeply, then there will be no Torah, since it will only be superficial knowledge.

Turning Ideas into Action ▶

▶ *Learn the process of achieving clarity.*

When learning, it is often best, even for someone experienced, to first get a clear understanding of the basic information. Take a small amount of the text and make sure you have at least a superficial understanding of it. If you have any questions, write them down, to be addressed when the material is seen a second or third time.[23] Once you've done this, move on to another piece of text.

Similarly, sometimes it's best to learn one commentary at a time and get it clear, before looking into another.[24]

▶ *Think it through with a chavrusa.*

It is usually best to study with someone else. You might find that sometimes it's a good idea for each of you to study the text separately and then compare your conclusions. Especially if one *chavrusa* is quicker or more

---

23. Sometimes it's worth continuing without spending too much initial time answering a question that has arisen. When commenting on a *mishnah*, Rashi will often say that the Talmud will address the explanation. The Talmud almost always elucidates the Mishnah, so why should Rashi make this comment? To me it seems clear that there is some obvious difficulty with the *mishnah*, and Rashi is telling you to keep going, it will clear up.

24. R' Elchonon, *zt"l*, said that he better understood the tractates that he first studied only with Rashi, studying them with *Tosafos* only afterward.

aggressive, the quieter study partner may never get a chance to think things through.

▶ *Relax.*

Stressful work does not usually produce beautiful and original ideas or thoughts. Relax, feel the joy of learning, and keep reviewing. Eventually you will see more deeply into what you are studying, and you will either discover, on your own, what others who came before you wrote, or you may even have an original insight that no one else has recorded.[25] The same process holds true in life in general, outside of Torah study. When confronted with a problem, don't search too nervously or excitedly for a solution. Calm down, study the facts as much as you can, talk it over with someone else, and solutions that didn't originally occur to you often present themselves.

---

25. See *Nefesh HaChaim*, Fourth Gate, Ch. 12, where the joy that a new Torah thought evokes in Heaven is described.

When Enough Is Enough: Finding Satisfaction in Your "Intrinsic" World

How much do my family and I need in order to be satisfied, to finally be able to declare, "I have enough"? We certainly don't need everything we are encouraged to have by the media: a cruise vacation to Alaska, yet another top-of-the-line gadget, the newest model in light fixtures... How do I teach my family and myself what I need and what is extra, what I can do without and what is essential?

And how about when it comes to growing spiritually? When am I expecting too much from myself, overextending myself in trying to reach an unreachable goal? Am I encouraging my children to grow spiritually or am I just pressuring them, demanding more than I should?

The Esav mind-set vs. the Yaakov mind-set

In *Parashas Vayishlach*, Rashi points out the difference between the way Esav speaks, "I have so much — more than I need," and how Yaakov describes his possessions: "I have everything."[26] Rashi implies that these two differing attitudes can be used as criteria for assessing if a person is evil or righteous.

Why is the difference in their descriptions so important? And what, exactly, does Esav get from having more than he needs?

We need some words of introduction in order to understand the principle behind these two ways of expressing our approach to life.

Relative worlds vs. intrinsic worlds

There is a huge difference between whether a person lives in a relative world or in an intrinsic one. A relative world is created through comparing to others; an intrinsic world focuses only on who we are, without reference to anyone else. To give a few examples:

1. Deciding that I am more observant than you are — without considering the differences in our backgrounds or in the education we received — is evaluating my accomplishments while living in a relative world. *My true level of observance is determined internally, intrinsically, and not by comparing to others.* When I live in an intrinsic world, the question I try to answer when I look at myself is, "Who am I and where am I holding?" and not "Why am I better/smarter/more religious/nicer (or worse/dumber/less religious/nastier) than him/her/them?"

2. Arrogance is a product of a relative world. The arrogant person always needs a point of reference — someone weaker or poorer than he is — in order for him to feel good; and if he finds someone who is better than he is, he is upset. *A true posi-*

---

26. *Bereishis* 33:9–11.

tive self-image, on the other hand, is rooted in who you are as a creation of Hashem and nothing else.

There is no arrogance in a positive self-image, just an understanding of Hashem's love for us. Humility is internal, intrinsic, a recognition of the gifts that Hashem has given me and the absolute difference between the Creator and myself. A poor self-image is comparative, relative, because I feel bad when someone is ahead of me.

3. Jealousy, the great destroyer of happiness, also is completely relative. Rav Shlomo Wolbe, *z"l*, defined jealousy as not appreciating what I have intrinsically and having too great an appreciation for what the other one has.[27]

We now have the beginning of the answer to why Esav needs to have so much, even more than he needs. Esav needs to have more than anyone else. It's the other one that is a measure of how much he has, not he himself.

The secret to peace of mind

The evil person's need to have more than anyone else (like Esav), as opposed to the righteous person who always feels that he has enough, everything that he needs, without comparing himself to others (like Yaakov), is at the root of the great curse that Hashem placed on the wicked: lack of peace of mind.

When a person has pleasure from what he has, from what he does — and from who he is — intrinsically, then he can have peace of mind. Rav Chaim Friedlander, *zt"l*, gives an amazing analogy:[28] when a cup is full, it doesn't wobble from side to side, but an empty one can tip back and forth.

Esav never feels full, because his cup is "empty": everything he has and is depends on what's outside of him. As soon as

---

27. *Alei Shur*, vol. 1, pp. 36–37.
28. *Sifsei Chaim, Middos V'Avodas Hashem*, vol. 2, p. 37.

he sees someone who has more of anything, he must go into action: he wobbles, tips over, and is pulled to and fro by his jealousy; he feels shortchanged. He has no rest, because he is constantly being pulled and pushed by his lusts, his anger, his jealousy. Sometimes circumstances don't allow him to fully indulge in his pleasures, and sometimes his desires find temporary satisfaction, but he is never at peace.[29]

The Alter of Kelm, in his *sefer*, *Chochmah U'Mussar*,[30] talks about the fact that the wicked are cursed with not having peace of mind. This indeed is the greatest of curses, because it prevents a person from stopping to reconsider his situation and change for the better. The righteous, on the other hand, are happy with their material lot and can focus on their service of Hashem, which gives their life meaning and additional joy. They are able to give to others, because they themselves are full.

The righteous person can grow, can set loftier goals for himself, because he possesses the tranquil spirit and peace of mind so necessary for effective self-examination. The wicked person, on the other hand, feels desperation and confusion, and thus it is much more difficult for him to examine his life and improve it.

The evil are always lacking, while the righteous embody the words that we say in Birkas HaMazon, "*V'achalta v'savata* — You shall eat and be satisfied." These words mean that a person will be satisfied even with a little; the amount he eats is not important. Of the wicked person, on the other hand, it says, "The stomach of the wicked will always lack."[31] The Gra explains that the wicked person is "missing a stomach"; that is, he wishes he had more of a stomach so he could eat as much as he wants. He wants to eat more and more, because it

---

29. As it says in the *Navi*, "'There is no peace,' said my G-d, 'for the wicked'" (*Yeshayahu* 57:21).

30. Vol. 1, p. 282.

31. *Mishlei* 13:25.

is the eating that matters, the pleasure, and not whether he is full. With Esav, with the wicked, eating is not about the food, not about how much he needs, and not even about satisfying hunger.

Rashi says that the verse "the stomach of the wicked will always lack" refers to the fact that the righteous feel satisfied, while the evil are not; they are still hungry even after they eat. "Is that all?" they ask. "I want more."

How we look at ourselves and our world

Understanding the difference between intrinsic and relative worlds, the difference between the satisfaction of the *tzaddik* and the lack of satisfaction that is the lot of the wicked, is not a theoretical idea. It is very much applicable to our lives here and now. *We cannot and must not measure ourselves by comparing ourselves to someone else.* We should not define success in relative terms, nor should we label ourselves as failures by comparing ourselves to others. We need to know that whatever gifts we receive are "on loan" and that we are expected to use them and be humbled at having received them.

This principle, that we need only strive to become ourselves, both lifts a burden, an impossible burden, off of us — we need no longer be someone else! — and at the same time puts a different, infinitely better, burden upon us: to become ourselves.

> I remember the first position that I had as a *mashgiach*, in 1976. I was told, "Be yourself." Those two words saved me. My two *mashgichim* were Rav Avigdor Miller, *zt"l*, who learned in Slabodka, and Rav Hirsh Feldman, *zt"l*, who learned in Kelm. I could have easily tried to imitate them — and failed.

Who am I — really?

Gesher HaChaim says[32] that the only true "I" is what I choose. *The real "me" is the choices I have made.* My choices are unique to me, reflecting what is expected of me, what I can and cannot do.

We run a race against no one; we should not define ourselves by the achievements of others. Who we are is about whether we are doing the best that *we* can do with the resources we have. Rav Shach, *zt"l*, once said to Rav Mordechai Orbach, *shlita*, "Everyone should want to be the best, but not better than anyone else." Only the wicked feel the burning need to be better than others.

> Rav Naftali Amsterdam, *zt"l*, once said to Rav Yisroel Salanter, *zt"l*, "If only I had the character of my rebbe, the heart of the Yesod V'Shoresh HaAvodah, and the head of the Sha'agas Aryeh. Then I could do so much."
>
> Rav Yisroel answered, "Naftali, with *your* abilities, *your* heart, and *your* traits, you can also be a true servant of Hashem."[33]

While we must figure out who we are and what we can do, we certainly can't judge if we are achieving our life's aim based on someone else's accomplishments, as the Midrash tells us, "Can a person see his comrade in the World to Come?"[34] The Midrash is teaching us that we can never truly see the "real" person — even in the Next World, the World of Truth. The "real" person isn't just measured by what he or she has accomplished, but by their level of toil and loyalty to Hashem, and only Hashem Himself can truly see this.

---

32. Pt. 3, Ch. 4, section B.
33. See *Alei Shur*, vol. 1, p. 38.
34. *Shemos Rabbah* 52:3.

"Good" jealousy and "bad" jealousy

Though we can't judge our success or failure in life by comparing our achievements to that of someone else, we can — and should — emulate a person whom we admire. We can learn from his good traits or his mastery of some aspect of spiritual life. When the Sages taught, "The jealousy of the wise causes wisdom to increase,"[35] they meant that such "jealousy" can be used as a tool to spur us to greater achievement. A healthy person seeks to see what the other person did in order to become great and then takes on what is relevant to him.

This is the difference between "good" and "bad" jealousy. "Good" jealousy is a tool, a positive way for me to achieve my own life's work and overcome my own unique challenges. I can appreciate what I have while looking at another's accomplishments. If I feel "bad" jealousy, I feel good if the other person loses what he has, and at the same time I fail to recognize the effort the other person invested to reach this place. I want his accomplishments — without his effort.

A modern offshoot of this idea is the phenomenon of "conspicuous consumption": purchases made, not from necessity, but in order to impress others, to make them jealous of you, to show others how much money you have. Statistics show that lower-income persons use a higher percentage of their income for such conspicuous-consumption items than those in higher-income brackets. Wealthy people don't have to flaunt their wealth and show they have more than others — because they do. Similarly, only a person with a poor self-image needs to impress others.

I know an impoverished cleaning lady who saves all year for a weeklong luxury excursion, where she is treated like a wealthy, pampered woman. It seems a shame to work all year for some imaginary honor.

---

35. *Bava Basra* 21a.

Turning Ideas into Action ▶

▶ *Look outside yourself.*

We should all learn to look outside of ourselves and appreciate the accomplishments of others. There are several healthy, beautiful ways to do this:

▶ *Develop a love for other Jews.*

Rejoice in their success, because it is also yours. This is especially important with those who are close to you. Husbands and wives should rejoice in their spouse's successes as if they were their own.[36] Just as the left hand is not jealous of the right hand's superior penmanship, since this benefits the entire person, so when you feel close to someone, you can share the happiness that person feels in his success, just as if it were your own.

▶ *Rejoice in another's simchah.*

When you attend any celebration, work to truly feel the joy of the celebrants and be happy for their good fortune. Schools have the opportunity to teach this to

---

36. My father-in-law, Rav Shlomo Zalman Freilich, *shlita*, was *rav* in Mt. Vernon, New York, for 57 years. As the wife of the senior clergyman in the city, my mother-in-law, Mrs. Esther Freilich, *a"h*, was interviewed by the local newspaper. They asked her how she felt about the fact that in all those years she never received an *aliyah* to the Torah. Her response was, "Whenever my husband gets an *aliyah*, it's an *aliyah* for me as well."

children when they attend a *siyum* celebration of another student or class. Remind the children to rejoice that someone else has completed some part of the Torah.

▶ *Find someone to emulate.*

Seek the character trait that a successful person embodies and think about how you can begin to emulate it. You may need to start at a very basic level, but it doesn't matter; you are looking for the trait, not the relative level. Perhaps the other person has developed his *bitachon* or *vatranus* (letting go of what you think is your due) and has achieved an advanced level in these areas. Your task is to begin from where you are, not where he or she is. Jealousy and despair have no place here; you should use the other person's accomplishments as a starting point for your own personal growth, not as an excuse to feel inadequate so that you give up before you even start.

▶ *Look to others — even those "inferior" to you — for inspiration.*

While you look for people to emulate, be careful when looking at others whom you perceive have accomplished less than you have: academically, religiously, or in their life accomplishments. To ensure that you don't "look down" on them, you can, and must, do the following:

1. Feel grateful for the head start in life that you had from your families and for your G-d-given talents. Recognize the people who inspired you and helped you to achieve what you have accomplished. This will help you realize that while you may feel joy at what you have done, it was accomplished only through the grace of Hashem, Who held your hand all the time.

2. Recognize, and appreciate, the efforts of others, even if they have, on a relative level, accomplished "less" than you have. Hashem has taught us that we judge a person's accomplishments according to the effort involved in reaching the goal. In fact, the Torah credits people for their efforts even if the desired goal was never reached. In the final analysis, we can never know who is more beloved to Hashem.

Elul: Small Beginnings

A lawyer once had a fool for a client: he insisted on defending himself in court without the benefit of counsel. Needless to say, he lost the case. We are not fools; when we have our day in court, we get the best lawyers to advise us before taking the witness stand. What you will learn here, based on sources from the best "lawyers" — our gedolei Torah — applies year round, but it is especially significant in Elul, when we prepare for the Day of Judgment, the day when we stand before the heavenly court.

Don't let the yetzer hara take you down

Elul is a time when we prepare for the judgment of Rosh Hashanah. When a person prepares for something, he shows that it is important to him. *The attempt to prepare for judgment is in itself a merit for us.*

As mentioned earlier, our first encounter with the evil inclination, the *yetzer hara*, was when the snake spoke to Chavah, the first woman. He made two claims: first, that she and Adam were forbidden from eating any of the trees in Gan Eden, and, second, that they would not die if they ate from the Tree of Knowledge. As we discussed earlier,[37] the Gra tells us[38] that these two claims represent the two ways that the evil inclination tries to ensnare us into transgressing Hashem's commandments. They are the two types of lies the *yetzer hara* tells in order to persuade us to transgress:

1. *He convinces us that keeping the mitzvos is too hard.* Hashem doesn't want you to enjoy life at all; you can't eat from any of the trees in the Garden.

2. *He distorts the truth.* You won't die if you eat of the Tree of Knowledge, he says, though that is exactly what Hashem said would happen.

Two misconceptions about Elul and Rosh HaShanah follow in line with these claims:

1. We need to become perfect — now! (But it's too hard…)

2. Hashem is pointing a pistol at us and just waiting to pull the trigger (a falsification).

Neither claim could be further from the truth. First of all, we can't be expected to become perfect at once. When someone feels that way, either he falls into a depression, gives up, or works himself to the point where things eventually backfire.

Rosh HaShanah is a time for recognizing the benevolence of Hashem. It is the celebration of the creation of a world of loving-kindness. We coronate Hashem as our King, and we want His kingship. In order for us to do this, we need to feel the love that Hashem has for us. We are all different and all beloved by Hashem. He doesn't expect us to reach perfection in

---

37. See Mind-Set 16, "Insider Knowledge: How to Fight Public Enemy Number One."

38. *Aderes Eliyahu, Bereishis* 3:1.

a day, or to achieve something that is meant for someone else to do. We run a race against no one.

> There is a beautiful story about a water carrier who carried water to his king in two clay vessels that hung on either side of him. One vessel had a crack, and by the time the water carrier reached the palace, that jug was half empty. The broken jug complained to the carrier about how hard it was to be only half as good as the other jug. The carrier told the jug to wait until the next day. The next day, as he walked with his water to the palace, he pointed out the flowers that were growing on the path to the palace. Those flowers were growing from the water that had leaked out from the cracked jug. A person never knows what his unique accomplishment truly is.

This is in no way a contradiction to the fear of the judgment. We need to know that we are not obligated to become perfect overnight, but neither are we free to do nothing. *The smaller the goal, the greater is our obligation to accomplish it.* At the least, we are expected to make a start, to take the next small step.

This, indeed, is the great fear of the judgment of Rosh HaShanah: Did we do anything at all to improve? Did we even start? It is for this that we are taken to account on Rosh HaShanah.[39]

So how do we begin?

Good beginnings

Be humble. Perhaps the most important element of a good beginning is humility. There is an amazing midrash that says that the fact that the *Kohen* is required to dress in the priestly garments even for the service of taking out the ashes that accu-

---

39. See Rav Eliyahu Eliezer Dessler, *Michtav MeEliyahu*, vol. 1, p. 257.

mulate on the Altar shows us that there is no arrogance in front of Hashem.[40] What I think this means is that taking out the ashes was a form of service, and therefore required the priestly garments, but it also carried a special message: taking out the ashes is an act that demonstrates humbleness, the willingness to do any kind of work, *and it occurs at the beginning of the day.*

We begin with humility, just as we begin *Shemoneh Esrei* by bending our knees, just as we begin our day by thanking Hashem simply for letting us wake up, just as we enter the shul by thanking Hashem for letting us in: "And I, through Your great kindness, enter Your house."

Keep it small. A person coming from a place of humility is willing to do something small and is not only satisfied with "big" things. *Something that is long lasting always starts with a small beginning.* It is arrogant to only be willing to do something big, as if it's beneath our dignity to do small things. Even small, easy things deserve our attention just as much as the larger, more difficult matters.

The joy of small matters. When a person takes pleasure from a small beginning, he can have a greater assurance that his beginning will not be short-lived. If small things make me happy, then my happiness is more likely to be permanent, because small accomplishments are far more common, and far more doable, than big ones. In fact, this point is so central that the Sfas Emes says[41] that we measure the greatness of a person by how much he appreciates small things.

Small, but central, change. We can't bring about total permanent change in a short time, but we can show Hashem that we deserve *middas harachamim*, His compassion, by beginning on a path that shows that we will indeed change. The change should be reflected in our dedicating ourselves to three vital areas:

1. *How we look at things* — that is, what's going on in our minds. It is our attitudes to life, our attitudes to Hashem, to

---

40. See *Bamidbar Rabbah*, end of Ch. 4.
41. *Korach 5636*, p. 113, s.v. "*v'al pi.*"

other people, and even to ourselves, that determine, in the end, how we live our lives.

2. *Overcoming bad traits* — Rav Eliyahu Lopian, *zt"l*, said that a sin is like a counterfeit bill, but the trait powering that act is like the printing press that prints thousands of counterfeit bills.[42] Identifying our weak spots, the traits behind our negative actions, is vital.

3. *Finding small acts that reflect the change that is going on inside of us* — every act we do helps us concretize and internalize that which we know intellectually to be true and makes it part of our emotional reality.

Let us take joy in small beginnings, and then we will have begun the process that makes us candidates for Divine Mercy.

---

42. *Lev Eliyahu, Vayechi*; see also Mind-Set 5, "The Path to the Next World: Character Traits."

Turning Ideas into Action ▶

▶ *Set your life priorities and form short-term goals to achieve them.*

Rav Abba Berman, *zt"l*, once defined wisdom not as the ability to separate the important from the unimportant, but to recognize that which is important and that which is *more* important. Our life priorities should reflect that which we know and feel are the most important measures of a well-lived life.

1. Take time to define your life priorities. Many things in life are important, but there are those that need more immediate attention, either because

    a. they are central to accomplishing your life goals, or

    b. they are central in keeping you from accomplishing those goals, or

    c. they are necessary in order to accomplish critical short-term goals.

2. Select one character trait that is affecting each of the above areas. This is best done in conjunction with a good friend or teacher or a close family member. Fortunate is the person who can happily and safely discuss this with his spouse, who is potentially his best and most important friend in life.

3. Select one small act that will help you work on these character traits.

Let's take an example to see how this works:

▶ *Take time to clarify your priorities*

A person has taken the time to clarify his life priorities. One of them, he decides, is to raise children who love Torah study.

Now that he has made this a priority, he has resolved to spend 15 minutes a day learning Torah at home with a sweet, pleasant tune. His children can sit on his lap or sit next to him, and he can lovingly hold them, but they must know that they should remain silent while he studies. In this way, he is giving his children warm and affectionate feelings for Torah study, while at the same time emphasizing its importance.

This person has also realized, after some thought, that his inefficient use of time is hampering him in realizing his life goals. A good beginning for learning to utilize time effectively is to make sure that he sets aside a specific, short time slot for a specific activity and consistently sticks to it. He can resolve to take 20 minutes of his day and spend it, consistently, on one of the following:

    a. time with a child or spouse,

    b. time for study of one specific Torah subject, or

    c. time to reflect on matters that he needs to keep in mind, such as gratitude toward a spouse or another important person in his life.

Here is another example:

▶ *Pay attention to your health.*

People often disregard their health. They are determined to start their diet or exercise schedule "tomorrow." Sometimes they have a chronic deficiency of sleep. While we can often "cheat" in the short term when it comes to our physical health, in the long term it will catch up to us, often with dire results.[43] If a person realizes that his disregard for his health is getting in the way of his long-term goals, he should begin a realistic program where he begins to pay attention to these needs.

One obvious area is eating properly and keeping an optimal body weight. To watch what he eats, he must develop the trait of restraint.[44] Much has been written about controlling our diets, and it is beyond the scope of this book to present a full program. There are effective techniques and, indeed, a lot of Torah that has been written about health and proper eating, both with regard to what you eat and with which intentions you need to eat. But, true to the theme of this book, here are some mind-sets that can go a long way toward utilizing what has already been written about the subject:

1. *Appreciate small gains (in this subject, it's usually losses!).* If a person needs to lose 30 pounds—the equivalent of over 100,000 calories—then one slice of seven-layer cake, which is about 300 calories, will be hard to resist. It will not seem to make much of a difference if he eats another few hundred calories, unless he realizes that 300 calories is indeed a lot when it adds up.

2. *Identify the benefits.* Consciously bear in mind, through ongoing study and looking at the lives of those who haven't watched their diet, the benefits of

---

43. Although the Rosh Yeshivah, *zt"l*, was an unbelievable *masmid*, a superdiligent Torah learner, for eight decades he stressed the importance of health and sleep. I even heard in his name that if a person abused his health as a young person, and as a consequence had less energy to learn when he became older, he would be held responsible for the *bitul Torah*, the lost Torah learning.

44. See Rav Shlomo Wolbe, *Alei Shur*, vol. 1, p. 147, and Rav Tzadok HaKohen, *Pri Tzaddik*, vol. 2, p. 79, for a treatment of the root in a person's soul that generates an unhealthy desire to eat.

eating healthy, both for you and your family, versus whatever momentary pleasure you get from the seven-layer cake.

3. *Savor the pleasure of rejecting the desire to eat the cake.* The beauty of this is that this pleasure can come from leaving over some of the cake on the plate or taking an extra moment before beginning to eat it (so that the next time you will be more able to resist it). Every small accomplishment, every small victory of intellect over physical impulse, is to be treasured and built on.

▶ *Take stock of Hashem's gifts to you.*

Rav Avigdor Miller, *zt"l*, says[45] that before we can ask for a blessed new year, we must first feel gratitude for the gifts of the previous year. During Elul especially, take the time to humble yourself before Hashem in gratitude for all the small and large acts of goodness that He has bestowed on you. Perhaps you can try to recall the difficulties and challenges that you had the previous year that you were, with Hashem's help, able to overcome. The best, however, is to focus on the myriad "common" gifts that we so often take for granted. Some of these are listed in the morning *berachos* that we say every day. Only after you have reflected on the good Hashem did for you the previous year can you ask Hashem for a year of success in all of the important endeavors in your life.

---

45. *Sha'arei Orah*, vol. 1, p. 176.

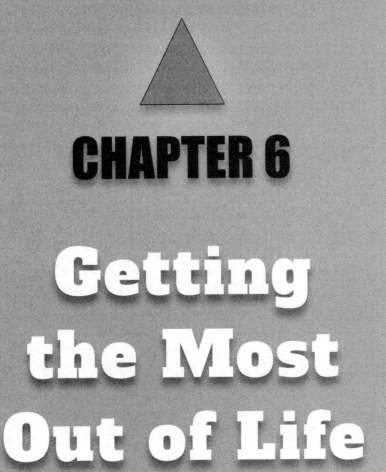

CHAPTER 6

Getting the Most Out of Life

Holding On to Things: What's Ours and What's Not

There are so many aspects of our lives that are important to us: family, health, home, finances, all aspects of our spiritual and material well-being. We do many things to ensure that these blessings remain with us: we invest time and energy into forging family ties; we diet and exercise to keep our health; we work hard to retain and acquire assets. Is there an overall strategy that we can do so that all of these remain ours permanently?

Understanding what is ours

If we want something to be ours we have to first realize that... it isn't ours. *To merit keeping any of Hashem's gifts, physical or spiritual, we need to always remember — they do not belong to us!*

Here are some examples of this principle:

Eretz Yisrael

Eretz Yisrael is a gift, given by Hashem to the Jewish people. In order to keep this gift, we need to recognize that it is not irrevocably ours. To retain our hold on it, the Torah commands us to keep *shemittah*: once every seven years, it is forbidden to farm the land.[1] This prohibition reminds us that what we think belongs to us really doesn't. Failure to keep the command of *shemittah* leads to exile, when Eretz Yisrael is temporarily taken away from us.[2]

This is also why, when the Temple stood in Jerusalem, the Jews had to leave their homes behind and gather at the Temple three times a year, on Pesach, Shavuos, and Succos. This was a fulfillment of the command to be *oleh regel*, to come and be in the presence of Hashem.[3] Rav Avigdor Miller, *zt"l*, notes that in this commandment Hashem is called "*Adon*," which means "Master" or "Boss." This is to emphasize that leaving our homes and fields behind and coming to Jerusalem was a way of expressing that we remember that we are Hashem's guests here.

When we recognize that the Land isn't intrinsically ours, then we merit to be able to remain there. This is manifest in the fact that fulfillment of the command to come to Jerusalem three times a year brought with it the blessing that other nations would not desire our land.[4]

---

1. *Vayikra* 25:1–6.
2. See *Rashi, Vayikra* 26:34.
3. *Shemos* 23:17.
4. Ibid. 34:24.

Wealth

When we give charity, we are expressing the idea that our possessions and wealth are not really ours. Hashem gave them to us as a gift, and we are merely the trustees appointed to ensure that the money is used properly. In fact, giving away the fruits of our labors — *terumah* to the *Kohen*, *ma'aser* to the *Levi*, and charity to the poor — is the recommended practice to increase one's wealth.[5]

Our families

How can we "keep" our families? How can we have a close, caring relationship with our spouses, our children, our parents?

We have to remember that our families are not "ours"; we must not take them for granted. Think about the "bad old days" — when you were not yet blessed with a person willing to share his or her life with you. Realize that children are not automatic in a marriage. Likewise, be aware that your parents will not always be here in this world with you.

By internalizing the idea that your parents, children, and spouse do not belong to you, that you are not simply entitled to their presence in your life, you will remember to treat them with compassion, kindness, and care — and you will find that you can "keep" them close to you.

Sometimes parents of newlyweds have to make a special effort to remember that that their children are not "theirs." Now is the time to maintain some distance and allow their married children to build their own home, while at the same time letting them know that they, their parents, are always there to help. If we remember that our married children are not ours to direct, we will merit to keep them close to us with strong and positive relationships.

---

5. *Devarim* 14:22; *Shabbos* 119a.

Our health

Good health and a properly functioning body is not something that comes to you by right: don't take your body and health for granted. Your body is a good friend, treat it with gratitude and compassion. Eat a proper diet, exercise, and remember when saying the morning blessings and during prayers to be thankful for the daily gift of health, for those bodily functions that work well.

Rav Avigdor Miller, *zt"l*, says that we need to be grateful even for *past* health if we no longer enjoy the blessing of perfect health, as it says, "They will talk of the memory of Your past benevolence"[6] — even for the memory we must be grateful.

When we appreciate our health, we tend to be more attentive to retaining it. Perhaps this is why Rav Chatzkel Levenstein, *zt"l*, told Rav Shlomo Brevda, *zt"l*, that reciting *asher yatzar*, the *berachah* said after using the bathroom, with sincere gratitude is a *segulah* for good health. Some people keep a small copy of the prayer in their pockets (double-encased to allow it to be brought into a washroom) to enable them to recite the *berachah* from the printed word.

Life itself

Even our lives don't "belong" to us. How can we maintain a healthy appreciation for life and utilize it for good?

Remember that our lives on this world aren't permanent. By acknowledging that our lives are not truly ours, by remembering the day of death, we get the real gift of appreciating this world. Knowing we are mortal allows us to utilize our lives fully, to our eventual, and eternal, good. It is the knowledge that life here is not ours forever that gives us the ability to gain eternal life.[7]

---

6. *Tehillim* 145:7.
7. *Gesher HaChaim*, pt. 3, Ch. 2.

We must remember that nothing, not even our lives, belongs to us, and use that understanding to heighten our appreciation for all our many blessings. At the same time, this point in itself shows us that people, sadly, tend to appreciate most what they have lost or are about to lose. We appreciate more the waning hours of Shabbos, the beauty of a sunset, or a loved one when parting time comes at the airport.

Several years ago, a husband who lived for his job and never paid much attention to his wife went with her on a vacation shortly after she had taken a routine medical checkup. Before the results of the examination came through, he decided that he was going to turn over a new leaf in his relationship with her, and during the vacation he gave her a lot of time and loving attention. Toward the end of the stay, his wife, overwhelmed by her husband's transformation, turned to him with tears in her eyes.

"Dan," she said, "you've been so good to me. Did you get the doctor's report? Am I going to die?"

"No," he said, "you're not going to die. We're just beginning to live!"

▶ *Show appreciation for the people in your life.*

We often fail to appreciate our good fortune because we are accustomed to it or we think it's coming to us. A first step in appreciating what you have is to thank those who help you throughout the day, even when you pay them for their services, such as the taxi driver or the dry cleaners. Remember to sincerely wish them a good day as you recognize their help. I've seen again and again that they really appreciate it, and it builds your character in a true and meaningful way.

Even more importantly, remember to sincerely thank your wife for her daily efforts in keeping your clothes clean and preparing your meals for you, or your husband for providing for the family and taking care of the home's spiritual needs.

▶ *Make Asher Yatzar meaningful.*

We mentioned reading the *berachah* of *asher yatzar* from a card. A next step would be to study the portion of the *Shulchan Aruch* that discusses this *berachah*[8] and really understand what the words mean.

The story is told of a student of the Mir in Poland who needed to travel for an operation to cure a blocked intestine. After the surgery, he telegraphed

---

8. See *Orach Chaim* 7.

the yeshivah, saying that the operation was a success. When Rav Yerucham, *zt"l*, next spoke in the yeshivah, he said that every student, after a visit to the bathroom, needs to say, "The operation was a success."

▶ *Treasure the gift of Shabbos.*

Take time, when Shabbos is nearing its end and you are more likely to appreciate this gift because it's about to conclude, to reflect on your spiritual goals for the coming week. Treasure the quiet time that Shabbos gives you, allowing you to make sure that your path in life remains a positive and meaningful one.[9]

---

9. See also Mind-Set 19, "Preparing for Shabbos: Keep It Holy."

What We Learn from Trees: Vacations and Personal Growth

*W*e can learn a lot from the world around us. Sometimes even the most commonplace things are a rich source of true life wisdom. Trees, for instance, are there for all to see, but there is more to them than meets the eye. What is the significance of trees and how does this relate to our everyday lives?

A parable for man

In the Torah, the tree is a metaphor for man: "Man is the tree of the field…"[10] Without a doubt, the spiritual content of some-

---

10. *Devarim* 20:19.

thing is far more important in the eternal scheme of man's fate than its physical manifestation in this world. The Torah is directing us to see trees as a source of life lessons. Let's take a closer look at some of these lessons.

Always growing, always working

A wonderful Jew whom I know, a gardener, once told me that a plant that doesn't keep growing is dead. The tree is a high profile, aboveground, lasting example of one of the ironclad rules of this world, a kind of spiritual law of gravity: *if we stop, we go down.*

This is what the Gra said on the verse "The path of life for the successful one leads upward in order that he will avoid the grave below":[11] we either go up or we go down to "the grave below." Man, says the Gra, is called a "*holeich*," a "*goer*"; by nature he must move, and it's impossible for him to remain in one place. If he is not going up, then he is automatically going down. This is the very definition of our existence. In contrast, in the Next World a person is called an "*omeid*," someone who remains in the same place.

> Rav Avraham Pam, *zt"l*, the rosh yeshivah of Torah Vodaath, was an extremely active person, whose activities extended across the globe, in addition, of course, to his intense and ongoing devotion to his numerous students. When he became older and weaker, he didn't stop: his circle of activities became less wide ranging, but he kept going until his last day of life. His devotion at this time revealed, even more than when he was young and more vibrant, his unstinting desire to give to *Klal Yisrael*.

11. *Mishlei* 15:24.

Sometimes stopping

Although it's true that a plant is always working, its roots remaining active throughout the winter as it draws nourishment from the snow-covered ground, aboveground trees "take vacations" — and these vacations are necessary. This same gardener told me that in Florida, if the winter is too warm, the orange trees will not produce the same quality fruit, because the warm weather keeps them going, constantly working, all the time. They are lacking the "rest" that winter provides and have less "energy" to produce luscious fruit.

Everyone needs to stop at some point. When asked whether camp playtime should be interrupted to allow a distinguished rabbi to speak to the campers, Rav Yaakov Kamenetsky, *zt"l,* said no, explaining that break time is vital. He pointed out that the blank parchment between the books of the Torah, where there is a "break," has sanctity, even though it contains no writing on it. They teach us that sometimes we need to stop.

So how do we stop?

1. *A change of pace* — doing something different is a way of stopping.

2 *Resting the mind* — sometimes the mind needs to do something less strenuous.

3. *Remembering that we can't always do our best* — the Sfas Emes tells us[12] that perfection can exist only in the world of the mind, of intention; it is where we would like to be. In the world of action, there must be imperfection. To demand constant perfection is the road to insanity, because it demands that which cannot be. During the Egyptian servitude, this was Pharaoh's plan, to demand every day the number of bricks that the Jews made the first day, when people were still healthy and patriotic.

I once had a college-age student who had a perfect 4.0 average. I was tempted to give her a B just to take the

---

12. *Bereishis 5637; Shemos 5636, s.v. "vayedaber."*

pressure off her. Later in life, this pressure to maintain that average took its toll.

4. *Appreciating smaller, imperfect acts* — when you can't function optimally, remember that whatever you accomplish in difficult circumstances is often more valuable than what you can do when things are going more smoothly. This is a vital life lesson: we can't be perfect, on an absolute scale, always. We must appreciate — and take joy — from imperfect, smaller acts.

Keep growing, stop when necessary, and, like the trees, you will flourish.

Turning Ideas into Action

▶ *Value your "stops."*

When retiring for the night, or even if you lie down for a nap, take a brief moment to realize why you are stopping. You are stopping in order to be able to start again when you rise. This idea can transform something that you need to do anyway into an integral part of your *avodas Hashem*.

▶ *Stop before you start.*

Rav Shlomo Wolbe, *z"l*, taught that when coming to shul to daven, a person needs to stop in order to consciously affirm that he is going to daven. He should not enter shul and immediately begin to daven; he should make the conscious decision beforehand.

▶ *Pause in the middle.*

We know that our actions should be done for the sake of Heaven, for positive and altruistic reasons. Sometimes, however, in the middle of an activity, we can forget why we are doing it. This is especially true of things we do every day. It can be something relatively mundane, such as eating breakfast, or it can be while we are learning Torah. It is wise to stop for a moment to consciously reaffirm why you are doing what you are doing.

Warning! Danger Ahead:
Coping with Success

*W*e strive to be modest in accordance with the teachings
of Chazal and to emulate Moshe Rabbeinu, of whom
it was said, "V'ha'ish Moshe hayah anav me'od mikol
adam — The man Moshe was the most modest of men."[13] But
one thing seems to stand in our way: our past successes, whether in business, a profession, our family life, or our status in the
community.

Our accomplishments are legitimate, and we can and should
feel good about them. But feelings of pride, that I am somehow
better and more worthy than another Jew, and failing to credit
Hashem with my success have no place in the world of the Torah
Jew. Getting rid of those feelings, though, isn't simple!

---

13. *Bamidbar* 12:3.

Get off the roller coaster

Our emotions often don't see our absolute reliance on Hashem, particularly when things are going really well. How do we react to good fortune? Does it make us haughty or humble? Are we grateful, do we humble ourselves, or do we think that we are the authors of our own success and become proud and arrogant?

Indeed, we should seize our good fortune to seek a stronger connection with Hashem rather than take all the credit for our triumphs and achievements. People are so easily duped into thinking that they can handle things; they have to be constantly reminded of their reliance on Hashem. For example, halachah forbids us to eat before davening, because once we've satisfied our hunger we will feel that we can take care of ourselves, that we don't really need to daven. We know, in our heads, that we need Hashem whether we are hungry or not, but the emotion doesn't recognize the past or the future, only the immediate present. In our emotional life, we will feel the need to daven less when satisfied.

For this reason, a necessary element for successful *tefillah* is the emotion of *yirah*, which Rav Tzadok HaKohen defines as the feeling aroused when people recognize that they are deficient in something.[14] Similarly, the Targum translates *yirah* as "*iskenatun*" (אתכנעתון), feeling humility — *hachna'ah*.[15] When we feel that we are lacking, then we can feel *hachna'ah*, which is the emotion we feel when we humble ourselves before that which is greater than us.

Rav Eliyahu Eliezer Dessler, *zt"l*, says[16] that the main reason we have so many ups and downs in life is because when we are "flying high" we don't sense our need for Hashem, and then we have to have a "down" to get us back to our senses. *It is possible to avoid having the downs if we learn to be "machnia," to*

---

14. *Tzidkas HaTzaddik* 212.

15. *Targum Onkelos, Shemos* 9:30.

16. *Michtav MeEliyahu*, vol. 4, p. 226.

humble ourselves, during times of success. This is the hallmark of the Jewish people: "I love you [says Hashem], Jewish people, for when I grant you greatness you humble yourselves."[17]

We must find ways to grow the emotion of *hachna'ah* within ourselves without needing a down to remind us of our absolute reliance on Hashem. That would go a long way to mitigating our roller-coaster lives.

Humility enhances success

A person who humbles himself in his mind need not be a person whose accomplishments are humble; conversely, his humility can enhance his success.

> There is a beautiful story about a renowned lung specialist who, before making a diagnosis, would reach into the pockets of his surgical gown and touch something. When asked what he was doing, he replied that he was once called to an emergency where a young child made a frightful noise each time he took a breath. The pediatric nurse was confident that there was a specific life-threatening lung disease. But the professor could find nothing wrong with the child's lungs and was forced to call his assistant.
>
> The assistant looked at the child, asked for a tweezers, and proceeded to extract a whistle from the screaming child's nostril. "You may know lungs better than I do, but I understand children better than you do," he told the specialist.
>
> The lung specialist kept the whistle to remind himself that as successful as he might be, he was fallible. Every time he touched the whistle in his pocket, this specialist

---

17. *Chullin* 89a.

was reminding himself that he could make a mistake — and this kept him humble.

When Haman became powerful, he marked his good fortune by becoming haughty and exercising his power to take revenge against Mordechai. In contrast, after Mordechai was escorted throughout the city dressed in the king's clothes astride the king's own horse led by his archenemy Haman, he "celebrated" his success by humbling himself. As the Megillah relates, after completing his circuit around Shushan, Mordechai returned to sackcloth, fasting, and prayer. In the end, testifies the Megillah, "Mordechai became greater and greater";[18] he became — and remained — great. Humility in success — that is the formula for true greatness.[19]

Remember the old days

One of the ways of retaining your humility even when the world correctly reveres you is to remember your lowly beginnings, when you weren't as wealthy or successful. This was what Yaakov Avinu did when he came to the Jordan River on his return trip home.

Yaakov was very wealthy and had succeeded in raising an immortal family in the worst of environments. But he didn't allow this to make him haughty. He said, "The last time I crossed the Jordan, all I had was my walking stick."[20] As the Sfas Emes says,[21] even when Yaakov was successful, he still remembered, vividly, his humble beginnings, and therefore he achieved true, stable humility.

We do this every year at the Pesach Seder, when we take out the "poor bread" that our forefathers ate in Egypt. We may be

---

18. *Esther* 9:4.
19. See *Sfas Emes*, Purim 5634.
20. *Bereishis* 32:11.
21. *Masei* 5635, s.v. *"vayichtov."*

wealthy now, but we remember our humble beginnings and remain humble and grateful to Hashem.

I recall when I did some work for Dr. Michael Held and his organization, Etta Israel, I asked him to take me to Burbank Boulevard, near Victory Boulevard. There, as a 13-year-old boy, I was once a student at my rebbe's yeshivah, the West Coast Talmudical Seminary. With great sensitivity, Dr. Held left me there alone as I stood and remembered the changes that had occurred in my life for almost 50 years and how Hashem had held my hand throughout that time. I don't claim to be a humble person, but those moments drove home the principle that any success we have in life is from Hashem, and we have no reason to be arrogant about anything.

Turning Ideas into Action

▶ *Humble yourself before Hashem at the beginning of the day.*

One of the reasons we have so many bodily needs is to remind us of our fragility. When reciting the morning blessings, where we thank Hashem for the most common and elementary blessings, we can remind ourselves of this and humble ourselves before Hashem. Thus we begin our day, and thus it will be, with Hashem's help, one of great success in the context of knowing that everything we have is from Hashem.

▶ *Appreciate the "basics" — and keep on appreciating.*

It's a good idea for a person to focus on one particular morning *berachah* for a period of time. For instance, if you focus every day on the fact that you can walk, eventually your appreciation for your good fortune will become natural to you. You can then proceed to a different *berachah*. Don't be in a rush; the longer you can retain an excitement and an appreciation for any one "common" gift the better. The ability to feel inspiration from the same thing for a long time is a sign of spiritual health.[22] Rav Eliyahu Eliezer Dessler, *zt"l*, tells

---

22. A person once told me, with some chutzpah, that he does everything while Hashem does nothing. I said to him, "That was a great thing that you just did." After a moment, I repeated to him, "That was a great thing you just did." After

us[23] that the Alter of Kelm remained excited about an idea that he had, retaining that fresh excitement continually, for 25 years.

▶ *Remember what it was like before you were successful.*

We would all do well to remember the "bad old days," before we were blessed with the success we now enjoy, particularly the blessings we experience in our lives on a daily basis that we didn't have before. This can include being married, having a job, having friends, or having a nice home. We must be careful to focus on what we do have, not what we don't!

repeating this a few more times, I explained that I was duly impressed with how "he" controlled every beat of his heart.

23. *Michtav MeEliyahu*, vol. 1, p. 221.

The Road to
Self-Discovery: Chesed

S piritual retreats are quite popular nowadays, attracting people searching for themselves. In a quiet retreat out in the
woods or nestled on a mountaintop, they come looking for
inner peace. But the road to self-discovery is right outside our door.

Becoming a truth seeker
— through giving

The Alter of Kelm says[24] that since Torah is true, only someone who is "true" can comprehend it. *How does a person become true? By forcing himself to be concerned with the needs of
others.* This, says the Alter, leads him to love others more and
himself less. This process uproots the falsehood within him

---

24. *Reb Mendel* (New York: ArtScroll, 1994), p. 151.

and makes him a person of truth. Only then can he come to understand Torah.[25]

We see from this an amazing principle: people can only understand themselves by being givers. We know that in many facets of life we can only understand things clearly if we are not prejudiced against or partial to them. In the realm of self-awareness, too, this holds true: *the less partial we are to ourselves, the better we will understand ourselves.*

Put differently, in order to be able to give to others, we must be able to stand outside of ourselves. If we can learn to stand outside of ourselves with regard to others, then there is a chance that we can stand outside of ourselves with regard to ourselves as well.

There's a beautiful halachah in *Hilchos Tzedakah* that a person should be supported in accordance with the standard of living he is accustomed to.[26] If he is used to living luxuriously, even if he needs expensive food and a servant at his beck and call, this is a considered a legitimate need and the charity fund will support it.

> After the destruction of the second Beis HaMikdash, Rabbi Yochanan ben Zakkai was with his students outside the ruined city. An impoverished young girl ran up to him and begged him for a donation. Rabbi Yochanan asked her, "Whose daughter are you?" She answered that she was the daughter of Nakdimon ben Gurion, who had been fabulously wealthy before the destruction of the Temple. On hearing this, Rabbi Yochanan cried for her.[27]

Why did Rabbi Yochanan need to know who her father was? He needed to know what kind of lifestyle she was used to so that he could calculate the amount of charity she deserved.

---

25. For more on this concept, see Mind-Set 21, "Seeking Truth through Giving: Western Culture, Torah Values, and Our Lives."

26. *Yoreh Deah* 250:1.

27. *Kesubos* 66b.

We see that in order to help others, we need to get outside of ourselves to see the other person's needs. Even if these things are not important to us, and we ourselves have few needs, that is not what matters. It doesn't matter where we are; it matters where the other person is.

This is certainly not limited to money. Sometimes a person needs a listening ear and a caring heart. Perhaps you feel that his fears or outlook on life is mistaken. But that is not the point. Right now this person needs your empathy, without judgment; he needs to know you care about him and understand where he is coming from.

> A 3-year-old child who lived near Rav Elchonon Wasserman, *zt"l*, collected empty matchboxes. Reb Elchonon used to save matchboxes for his collection. Whenever the child passed by and call out, "Rebbe, a *pushkele*?" Reb Elchonon would interrupt his learning to get the matchboxes he had saved for him.[28]

Matchboxes were unimportant to Reb Elchonon, but they were important to the child. Reb Elchonon paused in his learning, which was of vital importance to him, in order to give a little child empty matchboxes.

This point, especially with children, can't be overemphasized. We can easily brush away the things that are important to them as being insignificant, since we know that they are "really" unimportant. But if we love them, what's important to them is important to us.

Try to get into the child's world. When a child falls, he may scream hysterically from his wound, never matter if you need a microscope to see it. A mother will take her child by the hand and give the "boo-boo" a kiss. She understands that the child needs her to pay attention to his distress, even if it isn't about something "real."

---

28. *Reb Elchonon* (New York: ArtScroll, 1982), p. 171.

Being immune to the two lies

There is a phrase — actually, a mind-set — that I believe can transform a person's life: *I can think about how I feel, or I can think about how you feel, but I can't do both at the same time.* Certainly, your own feelings are important, but a mature, giving person can first let someone else's feelings in and then see what's going on inside himself. Often, understanding what the other person is feeling will change, for the better, what I am feeling.

A person who is a giver isn't thinking just about how *he* feels, and this gives him an enormous edge in many important areas of life.

As we have said before,[29] the *yetzer hara* tries to tell a person that he can't, or shouldn't, keep the Torah for two reasons: either it's too hard to do what Hashem wants, or it's not true that we are not allowed to do it.[30]

A person who can get outside of himself will be saved from these two mistakes. He will be able to see things clearly. The surrounding world will not sway him; he will not accept that doing what is right is too hard, nor will he be misled by distortions.

When we begin with *chesed*, we can get out of ourselves and see what the other person needs. This will reinforce our trait of truth, and we will begin to discover our true selves.

---

29. See Mind-Set 16, "Insider Knowledge: How to Fight Public Enemy Number One."

30. Similarly, the Chafetz Chaim says, in *Shemiras HaLashon*, that the *yetzer hara* gives two arguments to entice us to speak *lashon hara*: either that it's too hard to keep, or that what we want to say isn't "really" *lashon hara*.

Turning Ideas into Action▶

▶ *Develop a greater sensitivity to other's feelings.*

When I was a Rebbe in Aish HaTorah, I began counseling boys who were dating. I asked the rosh yeshivah, Rav Noach Weinberg, *zt"l*, if he had any advice for me. What he told me was simple but ingenious (as many ingenious things are!). Teach them, he said, to notice other people's faces. Are they happy or sad? Is there something on their minds?

An unmarried man is accustomed to living for himself. He always looks for what's in his best interests, and this is understandable. When he marries, however, he will need to know someone else is there. (I will add: Not only there, but her needs come before his!) Therefore, a *bachur* needs to look at the faces of people and notice their state of mind.

What Rav Noach, *zt"l*, wanted to do was sensitize boys to the fact that there are others outside themselves.

This approach, I think, has all the attributes of a good exercise:

1. It's simple to carry out.
2. It's measurable — did I do it or didn't I?
3. It's something I should be doing anyway, even if I'm not looking to get married; we all need to be sensitive to the feelings of others.

4. It directly addresses what I'm trying to accomplish.

In the spirit of Rav Noach's advice, I want to carry it further to include the following steps:

1. After noticing whether the person is happy or sad, care about that person's state of mind; feel his happiness or his sadness, and then,

2. pray for that person; ask Hashem to help him in his difficult situation.[31] Also,

3. think about whether there is some concrete way of helping that person in his difficulty, or sharing in his joy, even if it's just a word of encouragement or wishing him a heartfelt mazel tov.

---

31. I heard from Rav Avigdor Miller, *zt"l*, that when hearing the siren of an ambulance, one should stop and pray for the person being transported to the hospital; after all, someone's life may be at stake.

Afterword

We live in a time when people avoid doing hard things. Happiness is seen as a goal when in reality it's an asset that gives us energy to build meaningful lives — especially when we achieve difficult things. Enjoy has become synonymous with good. If we enjoy it, it's good. If not, then it's not good.

We even give this message to our children: "Did you enjoy school today?" "Did you enjoy your meal?" "Did you enjoy your visit?" We teach them, unintentionally, to measure how they feel about something by how enjoyable they find it. However, often acquiring discipline and accomplishing difficult undertakings are not enjoyable. Good character traits and Torah scholarship, for example, are never achieved easily.

Children balk strongly at doing things they don't enjoy. That's why we want to send the message, not that everything necessarily has to be enjoyable, but that *we cannot serve Hashem and live meaningful lives if we're not prepared to do hard things.*

The basic message of this book is that I am responsible for those things that I can control or at least influence. Our greatest level of control is in our minds — our thoughts, responses, and attitudes: our mind-sets. It is my hope that the mind-sets presented in this book will help us be able to give *nachas* to the *Ribbono shel Olam*, bringing us the joy of living meaningful lives in this world and making a permanent connection to Him in the World to Come.

No matter our efforts in any area, in the end we need to pray to Hashem for any success we want to achieve. It is my prayer that this book succeed in making a positive impact. Even if just one person has been helped by reading this book, that is more than sufficient reason for me to have invested in the work necessary to produce it.

This volume is part of
THE ARTSCROLL SERIES®
an ongoing project of
translations, commentaries and expositions on
Scripture, Mishnah, Talmud, Midrash, Halachah,
liturgy, history, the classic Rabbinic writings,
biographies and thought.

For a brochure of current publications
visit your local Hebrew bookseller
or contact the publisher:

Mesorah Publications, ltd

4401 Second Avenue
Brooklyn, New York 11232
(718) 921-9000
www.artscroll.com